THAT'S WHAT SHe SaID.

From the Stage to the Page VOLUME 1

A Collection of Stories from the Women of
"That's What She Said"

Produced by **Jenette Jurczyk**
Foreword by **Jill Pyrz** and **Kerry Rossow**

That's What She Said: From the Stage to the Page Volume 1

Copyright © She Said Press 2023

Cover Photo Credit: Darrell Hoemann Photography
The Virginia Theatre, Champaign, IL

That's What She Said Logo Design: Anni Poppen

Cover Design: Kevin McGuire

ISBNs:
978-1-960095-00-8
978-1-960095-01-5
978-1-960095-02-2

Disclaimer: The contents, experiences, and opinions shared by the authors of these stories are their own and do not reflect the views of The She Said Project. The She Said Project upholds that every woman has a right to be heard.

DEDICATION

To all the women who have said YES! to being a part of the She Said experience and spending countless hours discovering, writing, and sharing your stories on the stage.

To every girl, woman, person, who has dreamed of speaking up, speaking out, and being heard. Know in your heart that your story matters – that you matter. You have a seat at the table.

Let's do this.

ACKNOWLEDGMENTS

This book has been ten years in the making. Because ten years ago, three amazing ladies dreamed up the idea to shine a spotlight on women's stories and "That's What She Said" was born.

Thank you, Jill, Casey, and Kerry. Your original vision has touched the lives of so many.

Thank you to each community that has embraced "That's What She Said," as we've grown.

Thank you to the sixteen incredible She Said Sisters who are featured in this anthology. Your voices have the power to change the world.

Thank you, Kevin, who was there, behind the scenes, from the beginning and who has remained dedicated to showcasing these stories on all our platforms. Your attention to detail and passion for this project is unparalleled.

Thank you, Lauren, Allison, and Julie at Burning Soul Press, for guiding us as we took these stories "from the stage to the page."

Thank you to every sponsor, supporter, and champion who invested in our mission and made our shows possible.

~~Prologue~~

~~Forward~~

Foreplay!

(That's what she said!)

Dear ~~Hotstuff~~ Reader,

Before you read the amazing stories in this book, let me set the stage for you. Allow me to take you on a little journey back to 2012 when Casey Wakefield, Kerry Rossow, and I were dreaming up this whole "That's What She Said" thing. Rossow and I were neighbors in the small, but mighty college town of Champaign, IL, with young kids running around everywhere, and we really wanted to ~~get away from them and binge watch Homeland~~ do something good for our community. We made up this thing called the "Moffice" (mom-office) where we would gather with our laptops and ideas and pretend to work each day. We would often crack jokes that resulted in a side-eye and a quip of "That's What She Said!" from across the room.

In between coming up with silly skits and ways to prank our friends, we would watch our girls play in the yard and bond over our common worry about the world we lived in. That is the true story of how this thing began. We wanted to come up with a way to make the world a better place for them, for our daughters.

We thought if women could be raw and vulnerable and be truly seen and heard, then maybe our voices would pierce through the uncertainty. We wanted to put women on stage, give them a microphone, and shine a light on women's stories. ALL the stories – from the addiction stories to the wayward boob stories and everything in between. We would call it "That's What She Said."

We didn't know the 'rules of engagement' for producing an event like this. In fact, we've never been rule-followers to begin with. We just started knocking on doors and asking people to help us put on a show. And before we knew it, we were sharing a stage with 11 badass women, each with a story prepared to share that night. And it was a night to remember.

Now, hundreds of stories later, our mission and our community has grown so much that it was time to take some of these stories to the page. Every time we have put on a "That's What She Said" show, we are flooded with feedback from women who were inspired by what they heard and started exploring their own stories. We hope that you, too, will be inspired by the stories you read in this book. And maybe they will spark something in you that could make for a great story.

So, this book has one rule: to let go of the rules and let your inspiration take you. In case you don't know how or where to start, we are here for you. I know your school librarian told you not to write in books, but this is your chance to break some rules. We left some space in this book for you to add your own story. Take some notes, write in the margins, use a highlighter! See what comes up for you… it's not that hard! (That's what she said!)

Then share this book with another woman who will be inspired to tell her story. And so the cycle continues. Welcome to the She Said sisterhood.

You're Welcome,

Jill

Co-Founder of The She Said Project

Hey Mama,

When we first started "That's What She Said," a friend likened us to "the little rascals" running around with feisty energy, full of crazy ideas. Our excitement was contagious and when word spread about a live show *by*, *for*, and *about* women, it felt like the stars aligned to bring the "That's What She Said" show to life.

We were overwhelmed with offers from local women – attorneys, graphic designers, and housewives – asking how they could help. People kept saying "yes" to our ideas, so we kept tumbling forward.

We knew by the reactions of our speakers, our supporters, and our community that we had something unique, something the women of our small-ish town embraced. What we could not foresee, though, is how powerful our community of Ambass-sisters would become.

And every time I get caught up in the excitement of launching a new show or welcoming new women onto a She Said stage, I take a moment to remember the simple power of one woman's story. For the most part, these women are not public speakers or performers; they are everyday women like you and me. They are our teachers, our nurses, our neighbors, our friends. They are the woman who checked you out last week at the grocery store and slipped you her spare coupon for the frozen pizza you were buying for your daughter's basketball team. Everyday women sharing extraordinary stories.

I love it when we ask a woman to appear on stage in "That's What She Said," and she replies with "I don't have a story... I'm *just* me." It is like waving a red flag before a bull, because every woman has a story inside them. We don't just have a single story – over our lifetimes, we all have a thousand little stories. When you hand a woman a microphone, invite her to share her story, give her permission to be loud and proud, it's pure magic.

In our early planning sessions, we knew we wanted to create something we would be proud to someday show our daughters. But also, we wanted to create space for women to tell all the stories- the sweet, the raunchy, the sad, the inspirational, the hilarious, and everything in between. The women who have braved the She Said stage created a community. We could never have imagined how powerful this community would become. When we see what's happening in the world today, it is so clear that women's voices are not just being heard… women's voices are changing the world.

The She Said experience reminds me of the feeling I had as an athlete, the sense of belonging; I loved being part of a team. It was unconditional support, it was a sense of knowing that we had each other's back, knowing that our teamwork was the door to our success. Those were the days that made me who I am today, and I am honored to be able to create a little taste of that for the women of She Said.

Butt slaps all around.

Loud and Proud,

Kerry

Co-Founder of The She Said Project

CONTENTS

Welcome

Dear Friends,

This book is a celebration of women's stories, and we hope it's the first of many. What started as a one-night event in Champaign-Urbana has grown into annual storytelling events in multiple cities, showcasing dozens of remarkable women who shape their communities. And we know there is no shortage of women's stories to be found.

As we celebrate the first ten years of "That's What She Said," we wanted to take a moment to look back on all the voices raised, the stories shared, the lives impacted. Each and every story sparks something within us, whether it's recognizing a common experience or seeing a completely new perspective.

When I met the women who created "That's What She Said," it was as if the clouds parted and the angels sang. I found my purpose. Now I get to direct multiple storytelling events each year and work one-on-one with women and teen girls to help them discover the stories that make them unique and beautiful. I get to inspire large audiences to connect and to feel the powerful emotions that make us human. I get to see the magic that each woman possesses and encourage her to share that gift with the world.

The results are so powerful that we felt compelled to find more ways to share these stories with women and girls that absolutely need to hear them.

We like to say "That's What She Said" is like a window and a mirror. And as you read the stories included here, think about whether that woman's story showed you a window to something you hadn't known about before or a mirror to reflect on your own experience.

Then pick up a pen and write it down. Use the pages in this book. Use a napkin. Use the back of your kids' homework, we don't care. And make it all about YOU. Remember you are the leading character in your own story. And the more you give yourself permission to be seen and be heard, the more you allow other women to do the same. We believe there is room for everyone. The rising tide truly lifts all boats. And we are doing our part.

Is "That's What She Said" going to take over the world? If we are lucky.

I'll leave you with the question that I ask each woman who begins her She Said journey... If you were given seven minutes and a microphone, what would you have to say?

In Sisterhood,

Jenette

National Director of The She Said Project

The Icebreaker

By Uma Kailasam

This story was originally performed live on stage at "That's What She Said" in Bloomington, Illinois in 2021.

Imagine walking into a room full of people you have never met before. Everyone is talking to each other, and they see you walking in. Somehow, nobody makes an effort to smile or say hello to you. Some of them might even give you a glance but then go back to their conversation. You are left standing there wondering, *is it my outfit or is it my makeup or am I too overdressed?* Then, out of the blue, you notice you are the only Indian-American person in the room, and BAM! That's when it hits you why nobody is making an effort to talk to you. Well, now you have to initiate the first conversation to make *them* feel comfortable with *you.*

Welcome to my life as an "Icebreaker" in America, the land of dreams and opportunities!

Let me guess your first thought when you see me, walking into some event.

"She must be from a very conservative Indian family."

"She probably doesn't speak good English."

"She won't have a drink, it's against her religion."

"I'm sure she is a vegetarian."

"I bet you $100 she had an arranged marriage! Can you *imagine* some countries still do that?"

Well, let me set the record straight for you: I am as American as anyone can be. I came here 20 years ago from a progressive Indian family who raised their daughters like sons and taught us to be very independent. English is my first language, and I grew up watching shows like Knight Rider and Full House, as well as a lot of Bollywood movies. I like my steak medium well, *thank you very much*, with a glass of smooth cabernet. And I have answered so many questions about my marriage because the truth is, I got myself into a "Love Marriage" (as it's called in India). I met my husband through a common friend, and we dated for five years before we got married.

I was born and raised in Kuwait, one of the richest countries in the Middle East. My parents were immigrants, but we lived among a huge Indian population. Life was quite normal being part of the community. I got a mix of both worlds and learned Arabic, too. I went to an Indian school and always fit into place. During the Iraq-Kuwait war, we had to move back to India, our home country, and I continued my high school and undergraduate studies there. Life was good being part of a big Indian family: the amazing food, the love and pampering, and all the festivities. I got to learn more about Indian hospitality, our culture, respecting elders and cooking my favorite dishes as well.

However, as I grew up, I started noticing that my skin color was very dark, just like my dad. My mom, sister, and cousins are all fair skinned, which is supposed to be better looking as per the Indian standards. I was the dark horse in the family… literally. But my sweet dad was always so proud that I looked like him. Yet, his pride didn't matter to me, as I felt that I did not fit the norm. There was even a time I cried to my mom saying that she used white soap for my sister and black soap for me and that's why I turned out to be dark skinned. My poor mother used to feel sad whenever I said things like that and always assured me she felt the same about both of us.

She said she never cared about my skin color. But I looked different, and I always carried that insecurity.

My parents and my sister have always remained the most positive influence in my life. They always made me feel like a superstar at home. In fact, my sister would pick a fight with anyone who commented on my skin color. She was very protective of me even though she was younger. They focused on my achievements and my talents and always made me feel on the top of the world with all their attention. Because of them, I grew up to become a very confident woman, and after a certain point in my life, my complexion became a non-issue to me.

After I finished my undergrad in India, I got the opportunity to do a Masters' program in the United States. This was an exciting opportunity for me, as I wanted to break the conservative barrier that girls could only travel to places like the United States after they have been married. America was the land of opportunity and a country built from immigrants from around the world. *How exciting!* In my mind, I should not have any problem fitting in there because I would be an immigrant, too.

I landed in Tampa, Florida to pursue my Master's degree in Computer Engineering. I should say, it was one the greatest experiences of my life, learning a new culture, making new friends, and combining the best of these two worlds.

I moved to Bloomington, IL after marrying and spending 4 years in California. My husband, the most important person in my life and the love of my life, always encouraged me to be independent, follow my passion, and break any traditional barrier. We both love the phrase "When in Rome" and embrace the best from where we live and the people we meet. I love being part of the community that I live in. We are part of a big Indian community here and very actively involved.

My husband and I own a few businesses and we run a non-profit language school for Indian kids. We stay active in the community by being on boards of nonprofits and supporting meaningful causes. We are both very social and love making new friends. If anyone asks us where to find the best Indian food in town, we say in unison, "Our home! You are welcome anytime."

However, as I attend many non-Indian events or go to meetings, I started noticing that if I am going to a new place, not many people take an effort to smile or come talk to me. Many times, I have come home telling my husband, "I don't even know why I am going to these meetings where I don't make any friends. Nobody calls me to be part of any event they are hosting or a service project they are doing. It's like I am always invisible until *I* make an effort to reach out to everyone." It used to be very frustrating, and I could understand why many ethnic communities stay within themselves, because if you are not a white American, you don't have a warm welcome in a lot of places.

That is when a very sweet friend, who is *not* an Indian, asked me out to lunch and said, "I see you at these socials with your husband, and you always smile and talk to us. You are quite social and friendly, but why are you not flaunting your beautiful Indian culture at the events?"

I thought, *what? Wait a minute!* That is surprising to hear, after I had spent so many years trying to assimilate to my new American culture, trying to figure out how to make my Indian culture *not* an issue. I told this friend that when I came to the United States, the most powerful country in the world with the largest economy, I thought people would see me for who I was, rather than judging me based on my looks and skin color. But here, I get judged, all the time, because I am not White and I am not Black. I am BROWN!

See, I am a person who takes constructive criticism and will change myself for the better. My logical brain started thinking, *ok, if people around me are judging me because of my complexion, let's see how to change it.* But the reality is, nobody can change their skin color and their looks (well, unless you are Michael Jackson!) I can change my attitude, my physique, my communication skills, my confidence and so many things, but not how I look. This is how I have been created, and I have absolutely no control.

If anyone had control, wouldn't all of us choose a skin color that is more accepted? And most importantly, the biggest question on my mind is: *Who set this standard that only a certain skin color is what determines beauty or superiority anyway?*

I told this friend that it was very surprising to me to realize that educated people in top professions make me feel different, and that I don't fit in here. I come from India, a country very rich in culture and education. And Indians coming to the United States are highly educated and working in top professions. Yet, it is very shocking to me how much emphasis and judgment is placed on something that is given to you at birth, that can never be changed.

That's when this sweet friend told me, "Uma, maybe you should be the first person to break the ice and start the conversation in such situations. Then people will know who you are and will love your personality."

That is when it struck me, *huh! What a fun idea, Let me try this and see how it goes.*

The term "Icebreaker" sounds very cool and *chill*. But really, it is one of the toughest things to do. You need to be confident and courageous to walk into a room full of people and talk to a stranger to make *them* feel comfortable with *you* and accept you for who you are!

Those who know me, know I am *not* too shy to talk to or approach anyone. I could confidently introduce myself to Jeff Bezos or Elon Musk today and have a conversation about their space journey. But one good thing that came out of being an Icebreaker, is that I became fearless about being judged. I became very comfortable wearing my beautiful Indian outfits to any event that I wanted to. I started flaunting my beautiful Indian culture and inviting everyone for a traditional south Indian meal and showing our Indian hospitality.

If someone judges me based on where I came from or how I look, I start to pity them for their limited world view and knowledge.

So, I came from different countries into America, and yes, I have to face all these challenges, and I am able to accept them and address them. But my children, who were born here, raised here, in the American way of life, are also facing the same challenge. That is what breaks my heart.

VOLUME 1

Let me share an incident with you. My daughter's heart is set on a certain sports activity, and she joined a new center in town. She is the only Indian kid at the center that we know of. She is very passionate about the sport, and as parents, we want to encourage her.

We went to a social event hosted by the center for kids and families to get to know each other. Since my daughter was at the center for only two weeks, she was excited to meet new friends and asked me to come with her. We both walked into an area full of parents and kids. Almost everyone turned to look at us, and at the same speed, turned immediately back. Not a smile or hello from anyone. Many moms were sitting together, but nobody said hello or made any effort to offer a spot for me at the table. I thought, *that's fine, I am here for my daughter. All this doesn't bother me anymore.*

My daughter was excited to see a few girls who train with her and told me she is going to go sit by them. She went over and the girls just blankly told her to her face, "Sorry, we are hanging out and there is no place next to us." I watched in horror, and my heart sank when I saw how rude the girls were. There were *so many* empty seats next to them. I told my daughter we could leave if she wanted, I didn't want her being around such rude girls and parents who did not even acknowledge our presence. But my sweet daughter said, "It's ok mommy, I am sure they didn't mean what they said. There are some seats close by and I will sit there." She concealed her feelings and sat by them, still showing kindness to them. All through lunch, none of these girls turned towards her or even said a word in her direction. She tried her best by joining in to play the games, but at the end of the two hours, she didn't make any friends.

My daughter didn't make friends that day, not because she is not friendly or social, just because she looked *different* than the others, and nobody wanted to take her in their group. I admired the strength and courage that this child had as she somehow accepted that this is how she will be treated at this young age. I came home and cried to my husband. I said, as a mother, I just could not take this, and maybe she does not even have to do this sport.

Who gives them the authority to treat others this way? In what way is my daughter less? She is an American, born and raised here.

8

She speaks English as her primary language and our mother tongue as her second language. We participate in normal activities just like any other American family. She loves her cheeseburger and fries. She watches High School Musical. She is a Soprano singer and got selected for the school musical to perform with her beautiful voice. We celebrate Christmas and all the holidays here. She is so respectful of others' feelings and swallows her own feelings to fit in. What *more* is needed for her to be treated as an equal? I just don't have the answers.

The only solution I can come up with is to teach my kids to be an Icebreaker to fit into the American Way of Life. Isn't that very sad? It is very tiring and exhausting. The next time you see someone walk in who does not look like you, give them a smile, and welcome them to sit with you; it means more than you know.

Kids are a reflection of how their parents behave. Let's teach our children to make a choice to see people for who they are inside, not what shade they are on the outside.

• • •

There's more to the story...

I was quite nervous to present my story not because I was not a public speaker, but because I was afraid that I would hurt anyone's feelings. I was concerned I would offend others and point them out as racists.

The wonderful thing that happened after I shared my story was during the afterparty. I was hanging out with my friends and our husbands. Suddenly I saw a line of people who wanted to talk to me. There were two teachers who came up to me and thanked me for sharing my story, and they apologized for people's behavior towards me. And another person was crying so much that people treated me differently because of my skin color. She said I was the most beautiful person she knows. I was so emotional and down to tears already. Another bunch of stylish girls, who I never thought would talk to me, waited in line and then said how powerful my story was, and they never realized how the other person would feel. Since meeting them, they have invited me to many events including their family events to make me feel included. I was overwhelmed and emotional seeing how my story was received and made a positive impact.

The best part was when a friend messaged me on Facebook saying her co-worker had come to the event. She heard my story and was so moved. She was in a neighborhood where many Indians went walking in the evening. They would cross paths, but never talked. But after she heard my speech, she introduced herself to them, and now they are all friends, walking together. She thanked me for giving her a different perspective.

Another person went home and told her daughter about the story. The daughter knew an Indian girl in school who was always quiet and never mingled. The next day, the girl made an effort to talk to the Indian girl and now they are friends.

When I went to a birthday party, there was an African person from Nigeria, who said she related to every word I said and was in tears during my speech. I was in tears when I heard her struggles were so similar to mine.

Every event that I go to, there is at least one person who recognizes me from my speech. They come up to me and thank me for sharing my story because now they understand what others feel.

My husband said that I did change the world a little bit for the better. It has been the most emotional and empowering journey of my life.

Uma Kailasam

Uma Kailasam's mottos in life are "Live and Let Live" and "Live life to the fullest with a smile." She is always called the rule breaker in a good way, because she wants to inspire women to achieve their fullest potential without conservative restrictions and encourage them to be themselves. Her passion is to mentor women, teens, and young children and motivate them that the sky is the limit for their efforts! She is an entrepreneur and runs her own business. She is a trained Bharatanatyam dancer and loves to cook for friends and family. She also loves adventure sports and traveling to countries to learn new cultures. She is a huge lover of Bollywood movies and does dance performances with her friends at events. She is a board member on non-profit organizations like Baby Fold and Carle Clinic, and is a Rotarian. She lives in Bloomington, IL with her entrepreneur husband, Krishna, and two children, Rhea and Surya. She and her husband founded and run AKTP (a "Tamil Language school") to motivate children to learn Tamil (which is their mother tongue, and the oldest language in the world) to promote the language to the next generations.

VOLUME 1

Naked on Healey Street

By Kerry Rossow

This story was originally performed live on stage at "That's What She Said" in Champaign, Illinois in 2013.

My name is Kerry, and I am chronically awkward. I come from a long line of awkward ladies. I have a long history of awkward moments and bringing shame upon my family. But when I turned 40, I decided to stop battling the awkward, and I was going to just let my freak flag fly - loud and proud.

You never know where these moments are going to happen to you. For me, one particularly awkward moment took place at our YMCA. My husband and I had taken our four monkeys to play basketball and to enjoy a family swim night. Which, let me tell you, family swim night? That is code for Public Family Squabbling. As we got to the door, my husband said some beautiful words to me, "I will take the kids home so you can stay here and have some alone time."

And so, at top speed, I sprinted to the locker room. In my sprint toward freedom, I forgot to get the gym bag from him - the gym bag that had my skirted swimsuit (that I swore I would never own). My suit was already in my swagger wagon on its way home.

I stood there having this mental argument with myself. I *really* wanted alone time. But I *really* did not want to join the Naked Locker Room Ladies Club. You know who those ladies are. They stand around in the locker room and they chit chat, wearing only a smile. And they do their pre-workout stretches. You can't unsee that.

I did not want to join that club. But nevertheless, I persisted. Throwing caution to the wind – and my clothes – I got into that hot tub. Naked. It was gloriously relaxing… for 39 seconds.

Into the locker room came Mrs. Stepford, perfectly coiffed and in her very appropriate tankini. Being the ninja I am, I quickly positioned myself so that she would be shielded from my full frontal. But my plan backfired, because the unsuspecting Mrs. Stepford climbed into the hot tub. I saw the horror register on her face.

We both stared at the walls for an answer. She lasted approximately nine seconds before she bolted, but she did not warn Ms. 19-year-old, hard-body, swimmer/trainer-type who was entering the danger zone. So, in came Ms. Hardbody. She did not have the courtesy that Mrs. Stepford had to avert her stare. Her eyes locked right on my 36 Longs.

There is no etiquette protocol to follow in this situation. I considered going all gangsta with, "You want a piece of this?" but that felt too creepy. And then I thought I could just go sort of bitter and sad: "This is going to happen to your body one day too. You're looking into a mirror, sweetheart. Your day is coming."

I took the good manners approach but apparently saying, "You're welcome" was the wrong call.

No time to make amends because the locker room door opened AGAIN! Are you kidding me YMCA? Really? Are you on the intercom out there? "Ladies and gentlemen. We have our very own Naked Soccer Mom in the hot tub tonight!"

I should have just stayed put, waited everyone out. I know that *now*. But being the Queen of Impulsivity and Awkward Moments, I freaked my freak. As I was leaping over Ms. Hardbody, I saw that she threw her hands up in a protective movement. I still don't know if she was trying to shield her eyes or if she was guarding herself from a loose boob.

So much for alone time. For days after this, every time I thought of it, I wanted to throw up. I knew I couldn't let it fester. I vowed to let my freak flag fly from here on out and speak my truth! When I told my sisters and gal-pals, I felt like a weight was lifted! I could continue to be horrified and never show my face (or boobs) at the YMCA again, or I could own my experience.

There is great relief in the telling of our stories to each other.

So, here's the takeaway: find your peeps, your posse, your tribe, whatever. Find those women who make you laugh.

My friends and I formed a neighborhood mom office, and we call it The Moffice. We show up every day with our laptops and our to-do lists. Some days we work in silence. And some days, we dance to 80s music. Some days we play pranks on the people who had the nerve to not show up that day. But every day, we laugh.

And last year, I made a bold statement in that moffice to my moffice-mates. I was working on a big project and I said, "If that thing happens, I'm going to run naked down Healey Street."

Of course, that thing happened, and my moffice-mates held me to my word. They reminded me of my commitment to fly my freak flag.

So, on a cold January morning, with snow on the ground, my friends lined Healey Street with their swagger wagons, and I dropped my parka. I took the coldest twenty-yard dash of my life.

And, as it was happening, I knew that this was a story I would tell my girls someday. Not today, but one day far from now. I will tell my girls, "find those women who will line the streets on a cold January morning to cheer you on. Find those women who will hold you to your word. Find those women who will remind you that you wanted to write that book or run that marathon or stand on that stage. Find those women who will fly their freak flag right next to yours."

Loud and proud, ladies.

Kerry Rossow

Kerry Rossow is the proud co-founder of The She Said Project. After eighteen years in the classroom, Kerry Rossow left teaching and found her writing voice on her blog, HouseTalkN. Sharing her life shenanigans, Kerry became a weekly columnist at In The Powder Room. In 2013, following the motto "leap and the net will appear," Kerry joined a service trip to Haiti, became a published author of the bestselling anthologies, I Just Want To Pee Alone, You Have Lipstick on Your Teeth, and Will Work For Apples, and took to the stage as part of the casts in Listen To Your Mother 2013 and 2014. Her writing has been featured on The Huffington Post, Scary Mommy, and Rants From Mommyland. She has come full circle and returned to a leadership position at the Montessori School of Champaign-Urbana. Her journey with She Said continues as the co-host of The She Said Project Podcast where she gets to yuk it up with some amazing ladies. Kerry lives in Illinois with her patient husband, her embarrassed children, and her naughty dog. She is the mom that makes you feel better about yourself.

Title IX Gave Me My Wings

By Kelly Hill

This story was originally performed live on stage at "That's What She Said" in Champaign, Illinois in 2020.

In the summer of 1974, who knew the battle for girls and women in sports was just heating up!

Title IX had been passed by the U.S. Congress and signed into law by President Richard Nixon stating that no person, regardless of gender, could be discriminated against in any educational institution which received federal funds. And so, the battle began in earnest for girls to play sports for real.

I was a high school sophomore looking for an opportunity to play the sports I loved, just like my male friends. But not everyone thought that girls competing in sports was a great idea. After all, it takes money to have teams, uniforms, coaches, and bus trips... Why would taxpayers want to spend money on girls' sports which had no future, or cultural relevance, at the time?

And so, I played with the guys. In elementary school recess I got picked first – because I was pretty good. In middle school, our games continued during lunchtime on the playground, and I was always the *only* girl. Every day, I made sure to have my shorts on under my skirt... so I could jump into the game and not be left out because "She was changing!".

With no middle school girls' sports, I knew my chance to play on a team had to wait until high school where the school board had promised they would be fielding the first girls' volleyball and basketball teams at our high school. The opportunity to be part of a team, to be a leader, made me feel whole and alive. I loved the exhilaration of a great pass on the fast break and the thrill of swishing the nets with a long shot on the baseline. I *loved* wearing a real uniform, even if the inseam on my shorts was only three inches. And, we all wore original Chuck Taylors (before they were even a fashion statement).

This probably doesn't seem very remarkable to most, but in the mid 70's, women were NOT championed in team sports. There were figure skaters and gymnasts, but even tennis players like Billie Jean King didn't get much respect.

Typically, those of us who loved the camaraderie and messy-but-magical chemistry of team sports were on the outside; too masculine, too aggressive, and certainly misguided in knowing our future place in the world.

But when Title IX opened the door, I suddenly had opportunities to experience the world in a new way. Excelling on a team and developing my leadership abilities led to varsity letters, an athletic scholarship, college coaching jobs, and now, college officiating. The self-confidence that grew with my commitment to this sport, set the bar for everything that was to come of my future. What I didn't know, was how homophobia would affect *every one* of these experiences.

After high school, I left home with a basketball scholarship to play at the University of Southern California, and quickly realized I had a lot to learn about how I was expected to present myself on a women's college basketball team. On our first road trip, we were issued Bobbie Brooks seafoam green blazers, polyester button up blouses, knee length wool skirts, hosiery, and two-inch heels. Our coach passed it off as a "department policy" for team travel. But we all knew why: the University, coaches, and athletic department wanted us to look feminine, "lady-like", and most of all, straight.

What we looked like was a gaggle of flight attendants every time we had to put on those awful costumes. Our team of mostly straight women had larger and taller bodies than the normal Bobbie Brooks model, so the outfits were ill-fitting, uncomfortable, and terribly humiliating. This was the first time I experienced the realities of being a woman athlete, and how serious the world was in wanting to control us.

Somehow, it seemed to matter who we loved. After being told that we would be wearing these ridiculous outfits, I knew there was a deliberate effort to keep us all "in check". It made me wonder how I would ever find a partner who might want to raise a family with me in this absurd reality.

In May of my senior year, I was offered a basketball coaching job at the University of Nebraska in Lincoln. I quickly learned that with this role came even more scrutiny. As a college coach, I worked to knit together the unique personalities of 15 young women into a cohesive unit, but I never expected to have the parent of a recruit question my sexuality or my methods of managing a team of young women.

In the late 1980's, I was sitting face-to-face at the kitchen table of our top senior recruit and her parents. I had spent the nine-hour drive thinking about how important this player was to our program competing for the conference championship. Although I had watched her play and talked to her on the phone numerous times, this was my first in-person meeting with her and her family.

So, I launched into how much I admired her competitiveness, and described how she would fit into our style of play. I shared my commitment to helping her adjust to being nine hours from home and helping her find an academic interest that would serve her beyond her playing days.

After nearly 45 minutes of laying out my case, her father began by noting that I didn't have a wedding ring and asked if I was married. I simply said, "No," then stumbled into some apology of sorts for not having found the "right" man. His next question completely threw me off.

"So how many girls on your team are lesbians?"

He then made special mention that the other college coaches had shared their "No Lesbian Policy" and asked what my thoughts were on this. Incredulous, I simply said I had no idea how many lesbians might be on my team, and I didn't make it my business to ask those kinds of questions. I really wanted to ask why this mattered, but he quickly added, "My daughter won't fit in with a team of lesbians." My anger rose... and then my heart sank. I thought, *how do you know, and why are you deciding this for her?* I managed to return the conversation to scholarship dollars and housing allowances but felt completely flattened and numb. On the drive home, I realized that I had *no* power to change this type of prejudice, and I decided I couldn't stay in coaching to fight this fight. I knew ignorance and fear would continue to be used against me in recruiting, because it worked. This long-standing prejudice was not going away easily. It would take brave and matter-of-fact men and women to choose to live honestly. Unfortunately, the sports world was not ready for this truth.

In the 80's and 90's, the fear of losing recruits and coaching jobs was real. And yet I persisted to coach and dodge questions and situations for nearly 12 years. After motivating and supporting young women into adulthood at both the University of Nebraska and Western Illinois University, I finally left a career I loved and moved to Champaign-Urbana to consider how my partner and I might start to live honestly and begin a family.

We needed to live in a larger, more diverse city, a more open culture, with schools we could trust to protect our children from the homophobia that would be directed at them. We were determined to stand up to the fears and innuendo that had shackled our previous careers in coaching and raise children in a supportive and accepting community.

To walk away and abandon our coaching careers had seemed unimaginable. We loved coaching and connecting our athletes to their strengths while building affirmations for their success in sports and life. But we had been so absorbed in dodging the cruel humiliation of strangers who weighed in with their unsolicited judgements, that we had no idea how it might feel to live without the fear of losing our jobs. And it was terrifying to take the next step toward parenthood, when no one "like us" was talking about this.

Once outside of coaching, we decided to be up front about our desire to raise a family. We started saying *out loud* to our health care providers that we were partners, and we wanted to have children, and we would be raising them as co-parents. My partner was not a roommate or an aunt or a friend.

The nurse mentioned at one of our early visits that the medical staff had discussed our case and had determined which doctors would be willing to deliver our baby in "this case." In disbelief that some doctors would *not* be *willing* to deliver a baby, we decided that all we needed was one doctor; convincing the rest of them would be someone else's fight.

And so now, looking back at the realities of coming of age in the 1970's, we live a very different life in a very different time. Our two daughters are grown and making their way through the ups and downs of peer pressure, social acceptance, and self-affirmation.

Now 27 and 22, they have their own stories about being raised by two moms (but that's for another story).

They have thrived in this community that has embraced our family and supported the love we all share with one another.

Someday, they may raise their own daughters and face yet new challenges.

Thankfully, they can talk about what their mothers did to pave the way for them to be accepted and celebrated, no matter who they might choose to love.

Kelly Hill

A native of Boulder, Colorado, and longtime resident of Champaign-Urbana, Kelly was a four-sport athlete in high school, and played and coached collegiate basketball before "retiring" to a 30-year career in basketball officiating at the Division I, II, and III levels. She and her partner have raised two young women and her family enjoys hiking, rafting, skiing, and visiting Colorado as often as possible!

Mom, PhD

By Gianina Baker

This story was originally performed live on stage at "That's What She Said" in Champaign, Illinois in 2016.

I left my full-time job willingly to be a stay-at-home-mom on May 26, 2016.

I went back to work full-time on August 18, 2016.

I know that many of us with kids struggle with the work-in-the-home vs. work-out-of-the-home decision, or as some call it "mom guilt" – that feeling of not being able to do enough. I never thought I would ever be a stay-at-home mom. As I think back to my formative years, I was always thinking about the career in which I most interested, not thinking about raising children as a job in itself. Additionally, many of the women in my family had full-time jobs so staying at home was not common. So, you might ask why I quit my job willingly to stay at home with three little boys. Allow me to share with you a few fond memories that made me reconsider if I could be, scratch that, *should* be a stay-at-home mom.

Memory #1

My seven-year-old asked my husband if I was a "one-trick pony." Of course, I blame the lovely influence of the older kids at day camp. Where else could he have heard that?! Because then he went on to tell us that HE was not going to marry a one-trick pony. My first reaction was, "Oh my, he knows what that means!" He didn't, as we came to realize upon asking further questions, but it was one of the first times it made me think they were spending maybe TOO much time at camp. Besides moments like this, I realized quickly that there were many experiences my children were having at summer camp with the counselors and other kids that they should be having with me.

Shouldn't I be taking them to the library to get books, or on hikes, or to the park? Oftentimes, the day was nearly over when I picked them up. After some sports practice most nights, we would eat dinner and, too soon, it was time for bed. It left only the weekends to catch up on all the missed time from the week. It was the internal pressure and forethought of potential regret that left me thinking, what else was I going to miss if I wasn't more available for my family?

And for the record, the answer is, "NO." I am not a one-trick pony.

Memory #2

During dinner one night, my husband and I had a contest naming state capitals with our older two boys. They got to use the internet to their advantage. My middle child asked us the capital of Iowa. Neither of us could think of it. So, we asked for a hint. He said, "D." I immediately responded, "Des Moines," and received a, "NO!" in return. Dumbfounded, my husband and I looked at each other confused, and just told him to tell us the answer. And he said, "DEZ-MAHNZ." But wait, it gets better.

We got to the last state, Wyoming. And, of course, neither of us could remember the capital and needed another hint. He says "C" and again I respond first with "Cheyenne." I'm hit again with a "NO!" After giving up for the umpteenth time, he says, "It's 'SHI-KNEE'." I know what you're thinking… blame the school, but I won't. The administration, teachers and staff at their school have been nothing but amazing. Instead, I'm going to attribute it to myself. When I was his age, my mom stayed at home with my sisters and me, and I can remember us doing a word of the day. Oftentimes, I, too, want to sit at the kitchen table and go over their homework, like my mom used to do as soon as we got home from school. Even though I'd probably mess them up. It is clear that his mispronunciation probably comes from me. I recently discovered, via Facebook, the phrase is "intents and purposes" not "intensive purposes." This also coming from the girl who still says "hors-dee-vors" when it is really "hors d'oeuvres."

Memory #3

But then there was that one day I forgot to pick up my son from basketball practice. Not only that, but I was also supposed to pick up his friend, too. After another long workday, I was racing back home on my hour-plus commute, in the winter, to fulfill my duties as chauffeur. Reaching what I thought was my final destination, my husband politely asked me where our oldest son was at… *three times* he asked me this. Each time, I responded that he was at wrestling practice.

It wasn't until he asked me point blank if I had picked up my son and delivered him, that I felt heat rise in my neck and my face, a lump rise in my throat, and whatever food I had eaten that day flip over in my stomach. Not knowing what to do, I reached for my phone to see missed calls and messages from his friend's mom and my son's coach. Thank goodness his friend's mom is a pastor's wife and practices forgiveness on the regular. I still haven't stopped apologizing. Most of all, I was embarrassed.

As I experienced each of those situations, something was telling me I was doing too much.

People often ask me, "How do you do it all?" And honestly, I don't think I do. I have so many roles, so many daily pressures. Those that I put on myself and those that I've purposefully taken on. Let's see, not only am I a working mother, I'm 34, just finished my Ph.D. in Educational Organization & Leadership, and am raising three, no, *four* boys including my husband! With family about an hour away. I'm a daughter, granddaughter, sister, wife, mother, daughter-in-law, sister-in-law, aunt, colleague, friend, confidante. These phases of my life have ironically been tracked with the ages of my children. I have a moving-to-Champaign baby, a start-of-graduate-school baby, and a dissertation baby. It's easier to remember their ages this way.

Something had to give, and that's what began the summer of Mom, Ph.D. And I was ready. I had so many great plans built into our summer bucket list. I had done my research, printed off four pages of summer fun, and it was going to be memorable. I even got it laminated! Since the boys attended a program after school each day, they were not able to have playdates during the week. So, I was determined to make more playdates happen this summer. And the pool! We decided to get a pass to one of the local pools (because swimming pools equal summer memories).

So, how did it go, you might ask? Well, we might have crossed off one page worth of stuff and those included practical activities like watching fireworks, going to a movie, and going swimming. And we might have had two actual playdates that didn't fall through. And as for the pool, my research was not good enough, as we discovered our middle child wasn't tall enough to get on the waterslides. We didn't go nearly as much as I thought we would. It didn't turn out to be the memorable summer I planned.

Being a working mom is right for *me*. It wasn't that staying at home with my kids wasn't fun enough, it's just that it is not who I am.

Towards the end of the summer, I started realizing why my stay-at-home mom friends were so excited for school to start. I absolutely love my kids, but I realized it was okay for me to work outside the home. I wasn't looking for a job in the fall, but a cool opportunity came my way. Not only was it flexible, but it gave me the chance to showcase other skills and abilities. And I'll never stop working for balance.

And as we move forward with more knowledge and perspectives, I still remember the summer of Mom, Ph.D., and for better or worse, my kids do too! There are moments when I long for uninterrupted time with the boys, where there is limitless time to create unforgettable summers that they will tell their families about. But there are also moments when I reach the podium and prepare to present professionally that remind me that I'm supposed to be here too. I have other skills and thoughts that need to be shared with the world.

We are still writing our family's story but making sure to include adventure and awesomeness. I have no idea what the future holds… if this opportunity will present itself again, *or* that I would take it. Our life doesn't work for everyone, I recognize that. Our family has found what works for us. And I am still working on being the best Mom, Ph.D. I can be!

Gianina Baker

Gianina Baker, Ph.D., is a parent, community member, educator, and a researcher at the University of Illinois Urbana-Champaign's College of Education. She has co-edited two books, authored a book chapter, and co-authored several journal articles in her field of study. Gianina lives with her college sweetheart, Ron, and their three crazy, active boys. If you're looking for us, you can find us at a park, gym, and/or baseball field, sometimes all three!

Out of Control

By Casey Wakefield

This story was originally performed live on stage at "That's What She Said" in Champaign, Illinois in 2013.

Things happen in our lives that we have absolutely no control over. We have choices, but there are events that happen no matter what we choose. We can't change or prevent those moments. When I was 19 and in my second year of college, my life was moving along just like any other student. It was predictable: go to class, work at T.G.I. Friday's, and make new friends. I felt like I had a good sense of control on my life and future. I was independent and making my own choices.

My father was pursuing a dream and passion of his by becoming a master scuba diver and moving to the Cayman Islands. Growing up, my parents were divorced, so I lived with my mother in a small town in Central Illinois next to the other small town where my father and extended family lived. I saw my dad every weekend and he came to all my sporting and school events. He was the type of father who would push me on the park swing for what felt like for hours, go to

29

the local school playground and rebound my basketball shots, or play tennis even though I would hit the ball out of the court and over the fence too many times to count.

He taught me how to drive stick shift in my car on the lane that led to my grandparents' farmhouse. Our vacations together consisted of snow skiing, bungee jumping, white water rafting, roller coasters, and any other adrenaline rush activities he could find. I was a cautious and careful kid, so I always had to muster up the courage to participate in his crazy adventures. During those times, I think he was teaching me something I wasn't even aware of and maybe he wasn't either. Parents have a way of doing that. Those are the moments I remember, and lessons I'm still learning from my father. He still teaches me.

When my father moved to the Cayman Islands, I was very excited for him, and it was his time to go on his own adventure – to pursue his own dreams and adrenaline-driven activities. Although, he always liked to share his experiences and show me, or whoever would look at his countless pictures of fish underwater from a recent dive, or the people he was diving with. So, of course, he wanted me to visit him on my Spring Break and share his experience in the Caymans. However, I had other plans in mind, and going on a road trip to Florida with friends sounded more appealing to me at the age of 19.

Besides, summer break wasn't too far off, and I could visit my father then. He was understanding and continued to write, call, and say, "See you this summer!" So, on the Friday of Spring Break, my friends and I made it to Florida where we were staying with a friend's relative. A few days later, on that Sunday, when we returned from dinner, I received a phone call from my mother.

"Honey, something has happened to your dad. He is dead. There was an accident," she said.

I learned that the Friday my friends and I traveled to our Spring Break destination, was the day my father died. I was told he was airing up an oxygen tank, and later told an air compressor used in a World War, and it exploded on him. He passed instantly. Some bystanders were injured. For the next several years, I believed it was my fault and felt consumed with guilt. If only I would have gone to the Caymans on that Friday to visit my dad instead of Florida, then just maybe, my dad would have been busy picking me up at the airport instead of spending his extra time at the dive shop that day. Then maybe he would still be alive.

But you know, I can't change or prevent those moments. There is nothing I could do to fill the void of losing my father. The process of grief, the loss, can be absolutely unbearable. That feeling of unforeseen and sudden loss is something I fought for many years as I would replay the "what if" and "wish you could be here" daydreams. Those thoughts would circulate in my mind and heart and leave me breathless at times - popping up out of nowhere. I tried endlessly to fill that void and I didn't realize I was even trying to until I thought of sharing this story with other people. It made me think back to my wedding day without my father to walk me down the aisle. It was a "wish you were here" kind of day and I missed having the security of my father, his support of a major life moment, and ultimately the look in his eyes, showing his pride and approval on this day. That particular look in his eyes is what I missed the most, even to this day.

I know everything in him would have wanted that experience - to walk me down the aisle. I'm thankful he knew my fiancé and now husband well, as we dated halfway through high school and into college. My father would have been proud and excited for our marriage.

So how does one fill the void of not having their father at their wedding? We had a large guest list and invited almost everyone we knew or are related to… lots of extended family, especially on my father's side. His parents grew up Amish, and most families are large – his was no exception. My mother's extended family was extensive as well as my husband's. I think having everyone there for the wedding day was my way to ensure comfort and avoid the loss, but no matter what, it was still felt.

Eventually, I have learned to surrender to grief, to allow myself to feel it and accept it. There came a time when I no longer wanted to push or stuff down the emotions. I wanted to grow and decided to deal with the pain. For me, running outside was my therapy and as I would go out on daily runs, I could think through and push out the grief. Finally, I gave my grief attention and faced it because I wanted to be free from it. I no longer wanted it to pop up out of nowhere and so I ran into it instead of from it.

I became comfortable with feeling the grief while out on a run, allowing myself to cry through it behind the sunglasses. Besides, it looked like I was sweating - not crying. So, I surrendered to the loss and grief, but most importantly, I allowed myself to surrender to the good things in life. Taking chances, living on purpose, and pursuing my dreams, appreciating what I do have and being thankful for the family I have with me. That's what he would have wanted. By no means would he agree with my thinking that the day he passed was my fault.

I honor him by taking crazy chances and doing the things that bring me joy… and maybe an adrenaline rush activity here and there. I honor him by having the courage to take a risk and see where it leads. So, it leaves me with the choice to live intentionally every day and to surrender to past regrets, mistakes, fear of loss, judgment, and most of all, to being myself. His life reminds me to focus on what is really important in life. Showing family, friends, and strangers love, mercy, grace, kindness, and compassion.

Those are the things I can control.

• • •

There's more to the story…

A few years after the show, on July 5th, 2017, The She Said Project received a Facebook message passing along a message from a man my dad worked with in the Cayman Islands. It read:

Hello, I just saw a video with Casey Wakefield speaking of her father's accident on March 20, 1998. Long story short, I was working with her father that day when the accident happened and would love to share a memory with Mrs. Wakefield. As I have no contact info for her, I was wondering if you were in contact with her, you could possibly pass along my Facebook info to her. Thanks.

I quickly messaged him, and we arranged a phone call. He was able to share with me more details and circumstances about the day of the accident. But most of all, he wanted to make sure I knew how much my dad loved me. This man only knew my dad for two months and the thing he remembered most about Glen Herschberger – he loves his daughter. I am in awe that by sharing my story on this platform, this man was able to reach me, so that all these years later, I could have that moment of connection with my Dad. From that conversation, I couldn't help but think how a father's love and memory never dies...he is still with me.

Casey Wakefield

Casey Wakefield is a co-founder of the She Said Project and That's What She Said show. She is a visual artist working as a professional painter in Phoenix, AZ. Wakefield is driven by the pursuit of the creative process in any project she encounters. As a mentor for the Milan Art Institute, she helps others pursue their desire to become a professional artist. Casey enjoys running, hiking, and most of all time with her husband Fred and their children Jamison, Carlee, and Emma.

Afternoon Delight

By Mary English Enright

This story was originally performed live on stage at "That's What She Said" in Champaign, Illinois in 2016.

Hello, my name is Mary, and I am an addict.
But don't worry, I'm in recovery.

As an addict, there are big chunks of my past that are super fuzzy, or that I simply don't remember. But see, that was the whole point: I couldn't handle life the way everyone else seems to handle life. It was too intense for me, or maybe I'm just too sensitive. When faced with any sort of emotion, and I mean *any*, good, bad, stressful, sorrow, love, *any*, I couldn't handle it, so I had to escape. That's what addiction is: it's escapism taken to the extreme.

When first asked to take part in this project, I had planned on sharing the story of "My Last Drunk," when I assaulted someone… with a salsa jar. But then I thought *maybe* that's not super relatable to the general public. So, I'm going to share a core lesson that I took away from my addiction.

On occasion, upon learning I'm an addict, someone will ask me, "What's your drug of choice?" The answer is simple: "Whadya got?"

You see, in my active addiction, I would take *anything* I could get my hands on to take the edge off and give me a false, though comforting, sense of security and warmth. Uppers, downers, alcohol, street drugs, food, men, exercise, clothes, whatever I think will distract me from the way that I am feeling, I'm game to try.

And this absolutely, 100% includes good feelings, too. I can't handle good, just like I can't handle bad. And I've learned it may actually be worse.

Good stuff is scary. Good stuff can be ripped away. Good stuff feels like a tease. So, when too much good comes into my life, I tend to freak out. And yes, I know that doesn't make any sense, but not everything in life does.

Shortly after I got sober from drugs and alcohol, I began dating an amazing man. Today, I get to call him my husband, but at the time he was just my super-hot, ten-years-younger-than-me boyfriend.

Early sobriety is very similar to overcoming any other sickness. It's not an immediate "stop using and suddenly you are cured" type of thing. There is a recuperation period. Like, when you've had the stomach flu for the past 15 years, it's probably going to take at least a long weekend before you feel like eating chili cheese dogs and going on the Tilt-a-Whirl again.

That's what early sobriety is like, it's a healing time and, at least for me, it took a while before I got my strength back up to a point that I could manage my emotions in any sort of reasonable way. Obviously, when dealing with major addictions, the goal is to cut out the most harmful and volatile components first, then work your way through the less dangerous ones. So, drugs, alcohol, and self-harm were the first to go, leaving me with a nice little menagerie of lesser, though still necessary, evils.

Disordered eating popped up big time for me during this period. That's a pretty broad description, I know, but it's a pretty broad problem. I'll just say that I was desperately trying to control my intake, was unable to do so, and would feel extreme guilt and shame when I failed... so nearly the same cycle as any addiction.

THAT'S WHAT SHE SAID

One day, I was home alone in the house that I shared with my then-boyfriend and I decided, very innocently, that I wanted to have a small bowl of ice cream as a treat to reward myself. And prove that I could eat a small bowl of ice cream by myself in the middle of the day and affirm there was nothing wrong with that.

This may be true for others, but for me, at that early stage in my recovery, it was likely going to be impossible. Why? Because ice cream makes me feel good. So, I will use it until it makes me feel horrible. What happened is I had a single small, socially acceptable bowl of ice cream. But then I wanted another.

Hey, that's normal, right?

I thought to myself, *I mean, I think everyone who has a little bit of ice cream would prefer to have more than just a little?* So, I had another. And another. And then I just stopped messing around with the bowl altogether and went straight to town.

Before I knew what happened, I had eaten almost the entire half gallon. Then the shame and guilt set in, and I knew that my super-cute boyfriend was going to come home and see that I had eaten all of the ice cream and would probably dump me because I was gross and didn't know how to share.

So, I did what anyone would do in that situation. First, I consciously said, "Screw it, the damage is done!" and polished off the rest of the carton. Then I put the empty carton in a plastic bag, got in the car, drove to the store, threw it away, went inside, purchased the exact same brand and flavor of ice cream, drove back home and ate exactly one small bowl out of the new carton, to appear like the kind of "normal" person who can eat just one small bowl of ice cream alone, in the middle of the afternoon. I felt better, but not really.

My addiction felt secure, so that's a good thing, but I had also eaten an entire half gallon of ice cream and I felt really gross about it… and (shockingly) I also had a pretty bad stomach ache.

Now the plan was not to say anything when my boyfriend got home, because it's so *totally* normal to have a small bowl of ice cream alone in the middle of the afternoon, and if you look at the carton of ice cream in the freezer, the evidence shows that is all I had.

But for some reason, when he got home, I couldn't lie to him, not even through omission. Which, I'll tell you, is a testament to *him,* not me, because I have lied to a bunch of people in my life and not felt bad about it in the slightest. When he walked in the front door and said, "Hi, how was your day?", the very first thing out of my mouth was, "There's a carton of ice cream in the freezer but it's not the same carton of ice cream that was in there before."

After I told him everything, probably in more detail than necessary, *especially* since I was trying to limit the appearance of crazy, all he said was, "I'm sorry you felt like you needed to do that."

And it hit me, though not for the last time, who all of this was actually hurting.

Mary English Enright

Mary Enright is a human, which can feel terribly inconvenient at times, but overall is something she's pretty satisfied with getting to be. She is the owner and accidental founder of Hunny Bunny Bakes bakery in Champaign, IL, which has been a greater source of personal growth than she originally intended, but it's cool. When she is not busy dodging daily panic attacks at work, Enright enjoys going on walks where no one is talking to her, reading books that make her cry, and teaching her kids that being the weirdest person in the room also makes you the most relatable. She loves talking to strangers, Diet Dr Pepper, and the way a breeze feels on her bare feet.

VOLUME 1

Get A Grip

By Amy Armstrong

This story was originally performed live on stage at
"That's What She Said" in Champaign, Illinois in 2014.

Many know me as a passionate mother of four and an advocate.
Especially, as an advocate for one of my children, who has
significant special needs and disabilities. But what many do not
know, is that one of the biggest challenges I have faced is navigating
the world of a teenage boy.

My firstborn was laid on my chest moments after thirty-six
grueling hours of back labor. And I looked into the vast ocean of
blue-eyed, blonde-haired perfection, and our souls met. And I knew,
for this, I would step in front of a bus or a bullet.

Two years later, after a traumatic divorce, my sweet son, Chase
and I were solo, navigating life together. And I protected him with
all my heart. And this plan worked for about 14 or so years, during
which I remarried an amazing man, named Andy. We had three more
children together, and I thought I was doing well at co-parenting.

All children have their own set of special needs, typically
developing or not. Teenagers are a challenge under the best of

circumstances. And within the setting of a divorce, it can become filled with landmines and quicksand. I began to notice in every picture of my son and I together, my hands were clenched into him with a death grip. I sadly realized this was a mirror of my current parenting style because *I* was going to save him from making poor choices, and *I* was going to keep him safe with that grip.

In most post-divorce situations, instead of going to court to settle your differences, most states require parents enter what's called 'mediation', and that's how you resolve your issues. I entered mediation in early 2011, because I was going to tell some people what they were doing wrong and what they needed to do to fix it when it came to parenting my son. Part of that mediation process involved my talking with a therapist and a child psychologist. And I was asked to make what I like to call *My Angry, Bitter List.* I was told to write down moments when I felt my parenting and my relationship with my son had been interfered with.

I started that list with the first time that my five-year-old was kept from me on Mother's Day. As my list grew, I started to see my insults and injuries and pain on paper. I spent many months in mediation. What I learned was that I was knee-deep in a battle to keep my son safe. When, in reality, I was losing the war.

I had a Ph.D. in passive-aggressive behavior. I was your dinner party conversation killer. "Here comes Amy to tell us what all the kids are doing wrong…you don't want to sit next to her." I'm all in, I get it. I had failed Chase, most of all, because my advocacy looked very different with him than with his younger sister and the world of disability. Advocacy looks different in all situations. And sometimes it can look like you're giving up, when in reality, you're getting a grip. I agreed to my child leaving my home in the spring of 2011, and I sent him to live at his father's house full-time. And in January 2012, I trusted my gut, instead of my heart, and I cut off all communication with my child. Mediation had failed to vet a successful co-parenting relationship. I prayed harder for him during that time frame.

I forgave myself. I figured maybe he would understand when he was 30, when he realized that I was not the devil. My heart was broken in a million little pieces. And I really thought for a while that I might die from that sadness that sat in my chest every day.

THAT'S WHAT SHE SAID

My favorite author, Stephen King, once wrote, "There's no bitch on Earth, like a mother frightened for her kids." I *was* frightened and I *was* a bitch.

However, in the mediation process, I learned it's an inside job. The only thing I could control at this point was me: my reactions and my behavior. The person who had to get a grip was me, and I had to get a grip on myself. I apologized to my husband because I had the crushing realization that I had allowed outside forces to enter our home and control my behavior. I had spent 14 years being reactive, not proactive, and I recognized the symptoms and post-traumatic stress within me. I drew the walls closed around my family of three girls and the sweetest husband ever, who loved me despite it all.

I changed. I was the one who had much to learn. I made apologies, not just to my husband, but to friends. I made amends where I could, I owned whatever it was, and I apologized and asked for a clean slate moving forward. I still had a lot of self-doubt and fear, but I stood strong in my conviction to protect my marriage and my family. I started the healing process, ensuring that I become the wife and mother and friend that I needed and wanted to be. Which, by the way, is a never-ending process. I still have to be careful of my resentments; I'm still grieving, and those can control my reactions.

I never again want to hear my son cry the way he did on a March spring day, just two months later, when he called and finally, within the sobbing, uttered, "I need you, Mom." And he came home. Together, we began to heal. I have my son's full blessing to share this part of our journey with you.

Forgive yourself if you're a mother struggling to connect or reconnect with your child and remember to trust the process. Trust your gut, and never let anyone else derail what you know to be true about yourself and your child. Mediation is one of the very best tools for any aspect of life. It's not just for post-divorce issues, and it works. Most of all, you are not alone. Sometimes you have to take a leap of faith, when no net appears; you hit every single obstacle on the way down. You smash right into rock bottom. But then you can begin to pick yourself up, dust off, heal, and keep it moving.

I am Amy. I am a woman of faith, a woman of hope, and I wish that for all of you as well.

There's more to the story...

It took more years of hard work and love to get to where we are today. Chase and I had the most honest, complicated conversations during the fall of 2020, during which we mixed acknowledgments of truths, partial truths, and apologies wrapped in owning our bullshit. Today we have a fantastic relationship where we enjoy each other's company in various ways. He plays tennis with my eclectic group of friends and me. He spends time with his sisters, taking them to escape rooms, out to dinner, and giving them his hard-earned trial-by-fire advice on navigating school, friends, and, ahem... boys. I love how protective he is of them, and watching my children love each other as maturing young people is a beautiful slice of life that always makes me pause to drink it in.

Loving your children and parents is a lifelong journey that takes many twists and turns, but in the end, hopefully, it always lands in love. When it gets harder than you expected, worse than you know, and the darkest of pits is in your gut, remember to try to land in love. Love takes many forms. Love can mean letting go, stepping away, and taking responsibility. I prayed that my relationship with my son would heal once I released all notions that this child belonged to me forever – our children belong to themselves and their own path. I had to accept and respect, come what may.

That is the magic light within ourselves that is needed to guide the way home.

Amy Armstrong

Amy Armstrong is a community advocate, and through volunteerism, she works to increase awareness of disability issues. Amy is a dedicated mother of four children. It was with the birth of her daughter Larkin, who was born with Down syndrome and further diagnosed with catastrophic epilepsy, that Amy found her passion for helping families and individuals navigate the complex world of disability. She is the driving force behind Larkin's Place, the foundation of the Stephens Family YMCA, a fully inclusive recreational facility designed to support individuals and families dealing with life-changing diagnoses or disabilities.

Amy is a contributing author to Gifts 2: How People with Down Syndrome Enrich the World. Amy is a skilled public speaker and can often be found at the University of Illinois, Parkland College, or Illinois State University sharing her trial-by-fire life experiences with future leaders and educators. She also works as a business manager for *Chambanamoms*, a local web-based company, while continuing to serve on the Stephens Family YMCA Board of Directors, on the Christie Foundation Board of Directors, and as the President of the Champaign Unit 4 School Board.

Amy lives with her husband, Andrew, in Champaign and prides herself on her kitten herding skills of one son Chase, Larkin, and twins Brin and Erin.

VOLUME 1

#sorrymomanddad

By Lana Branch

This story was originally performed live on stage at "That's What She Said" in Bloomington, Illinois in 2019.

"Fart, poop, doody, goody, goody, hairball, KERTUGAN!" I have no idea what those words mean. What I do know, is that when my sons initiate this mantra, I am required to join in and say my part. My sons. Sometimes, it hits me out of nowhere that I'm a mom. After repeated failed IVFs and a successful one that ended in a miscarriage, the Universe finally said it was my time. On February 11, 2015, a three-and-a-half-year-old and a 20-month-old joined our family. Since then, I've doubled the kid count and currently have four boys, ages eight, six, two, and eight months.

I was lucky that my kids came readymade; the last one was still warm out of the oven at 48 hours old. Unlike most moms, I was able to avoid the stretch marks associated with pregnancy. All my stretch marks are courtesy of supersizing and beer. I was also able to avoid having to cross my legs whenever I sneeze or cough. My wife gave birth to four kids and when she coughs or sneezes, she has to cross her legs, and I laugh every time.

#sorrymomanddad

Dear Mom, on behalf of all your kids, I am sorry that we wreaked havoc on your body.

I knew that being a parent was a combination of love, patience, kindness, and selflessness, because that's what I experienced growing up with my parents. What I failed to realize was that the other side of parenting included being broke all the time, giving up the last bite of your favorite food, never having time alone, and, well, penises.

I'm an old school lesbian, and according to the "Lesbian Handbook," I should not have seen the number of penises I've seen in the last four years in my entire gay lifetime! I understood that with babies there were a lot of diapers and then potty training, however, with the older two boys, it has gotten out of hand. We don't live in a clothing-optional home, so we wear clothes all the time. But the first time I yelled, "Child, stop running around this house naked and put some clothes on!" I looked behind me, expecting to see my mom, because those are words that have come out of her mouth.

It was in that moment that a light bulb flashed brightly over my head, and I remembered the Universe. The same Universe who was once so gracious to bless me with the title of Mom was now laughing and saying, "It's payback time." I froze and mentally pressed rewind on my childhood and instantly felt sick to my stomach. That's a lot to pay back! I tried brushing off the feeling of dread, thinking the Universe could not be so vindictive as to hold my adult-self responsible for my actions as a child. I was wrong.

It started with the lies. One day, Dante came home from daycare when he was four years old singing an awesome song about the thunder and the lightning. He was really into it and sang it for over a minute. I asked him if Ms. Brittney played it for him at school. With the proudest swag and the biggest grin, he replied, "No, I made it up." I believed him for over a week until I heard the song on the radio. My first thought was, *how did Imagine Dragons steal my son's music and lyrics?* My second thought that quickly followed was, *my son must have lied to me.* It hurt my feelings because I worked hard to be that mom that they can come talk to about anything.

It wasn't the first lie, and it certainly won't be the last one. Thankfully they don't do it all the time; it's only when they open their mouths to speak. I truly believe that they believe some of the stuff that they say. So, to them it's not lying. Often, I bring proof to a discussion to show them they are wrong (because in my world, it's important to win every argument with a kid.) Even with proof, they will look me square in the eye and stick with the lie.

Universe. Payback.

#sorrymomanddad

Dear Mom, when you asked 12-year-old me if I put regular dish soap in the dishwasher, I lied to you and said, "No." While we both stood in the middle of the kitchen floor surrounded by bubbles coming out of the machine, I looked you in the eye and stuck with the lie. My rationale was that I thought the soap would get the dishes cleaner, but that was no excuse to not tell the truth in that moment. I wish I could go back and clean the floor before you got home. You would have never known, and I would have learned my lesson.

As a Mom, I have often stretched the truth or postponed an answer just to make life easier.

"Can we go out to eat?"

"I don't have fast food money."

"Can I have a sleepover?"

"I'll think about it."

"Can we have dessert?"

"It's way too late to eat sweets."

I respond knowing that I have a $50 bill hidden in my wallet, my hands are full with my four boys without adding more, and I have been dreaming about that pint of Ben and Jerry's all day long.

There are other unsavory kid behaviors that I try to curb and correct while they are still young. So, when I catch the boys in a lie or sitting on each other farting, I tend to channel Dad and let them know in a very strong voice, through clenched teeth, that their behavior is unacceptable.

One day, I walked into the playroom and felt a breeze, even though the outside doors were closed. It was then the broken window came into view. Since it was the second broken window that week, I could feel the heat of anger crawling up my skin, collecting choice words along the way that would soon come bellowing out of my mouth. To share those words with my sons, I had to call them out from wherever they were hiding. My intention was to yell their names loudly. However, when I opened my mouth the names of my son's did not make an appearance.

Instead, I summoned my three brothers, some cousins, and a few uncles. My inability to say what I meant made me angrier and I tried again, but this time, I used the name Willis Roberts. I knew I had lost in that moment because Willis Roberts was my great, great grandfather who came from Madagascar as an interpreter in the 1850s. I gave up and sat in silence collecting my thoughts, accepting the fact that the broken window could wait.

#sorrymomanddad

Dear Mom and Dad, I'm sorry I got upset every time I thought you forgot who I was when you called me by someone else's name. To a kid, when you don't say *their* name, they may feel invisible. Now I realize that's not the case. It's just so many faces and so many names to remember. Maybe I should use name tags like they did at my old job.

I worked in the liquid tank room in a candy factory for over twenty years, so I know a thing or two about chocolate. The first is every color of chocolate is delicious. The other thing is that as chocolate gets old, it may bloom and produce a white coating. My sons range from dark chocolate to white chocolate. The bloom on chocolate people is called getting "ashy."

I have made sure that our house and vehicles are equipped with all the right oils and lotions to ensure that three of my sons and I are always ready to cover our elbows and knees at a moment's notice. My wife and the baby are Casper-the-Ghost white, so she doesn't really understand the need for so many options. But if not lotioned up daily, especially after bath time, our two-year-old Andre would look like he fought with a bag of flour and lost. One day, I was lotioning up all the kids which included the baby, but I forgot to tell my wife. When she picked up Matthew, he almost slid out of her hands. It's embarrassing to take a kid out of the house with knees and elbows covered in ash!

Universe. Payback.

#sorrymomanddad

Dear Mom and Dad, I'm sorry for catching an attitude every time you fussed at me for not putting lotion on before leaving the house. The ash is real. I get it now.

However, there is something that I still don't get. Why did they always deny that my brother Carl was their favorite kid? I have a daily favorite and all the kids know it. It's an incentive for the others to work harder so they feel they can make it to the top of the list. If my folks had admitted I was just a runner up to the favorite, I would have had the opportunity to act, like knock Carl out of the running by lying and saying *he* put the dish soap in the dishwasher.

With siblings comes sibling rivalry: fights, arguments, and everything is a competition. I forgot how Mom and Dad made us stop fighting until a wave of memories washed through my brain while breaking up a fight with the two older boys. Tre took one last swing at Dante but connected with my thigh. The frustration ran up my body as my teeth clenched and I started to say something, but this time Dad's words tumbled off my tongue, "Do that again and I'll break your goshdarn neck!" The boys stopped in their tracks and again I froze as 14-year-old me looked around waiting for the follow up words, "Go to your room and don't even think about coming out" hung, not in the air, but in my soul.

#sorrymomanddad

Dear Dad, I'm sorry that we pushed you to the point of almost cussing. It got our attention as it got my sons' attention, and your angry tagline lives on.

Parenting is not for everyone. It's an acquired taste that one should consider as they peruse the menu of life's choices. For example, not everyone will run to the buffet to grab Rocky Mountain Oysters, which to some are considered a delicacy. Bull testicles? It's a hard pass for me. For those who choose to put bull testicles in their mouth, I applaud you.

For those of us who choose to parent through birth, fostering, or adoption, I feel you. It's hard! Being responsible for a living, breathing being is scary. Mom still talks about holding a mirror to our mouths while we were sleeping and not leaving until it fogged over. It's not a joke. I have tiptoed into my children's room at night just to witness the rise and fall of their chests, to stand in that peace and quiet, to smile at their angelic and beautiful faces, and to congratulate myself for making it through another day. However, before I reach their beds, I usually trip over a toy, run into a dresser, and yell. This tends to disturb their sleep and wake them up. When that happens, I can leave the room satisfied that they are still alive and breathing.

#sorrymomanddad that I kept my room a mess.

#sorrymomanddad for playing with the box the toy came in more than the toy.

#sorrymomanddad for being so extra when your friends came over making it seem like I had no home training.

#sorrymomanddad that I ever doubted you had enough love to go around.

We all grow up and grow out of kid habits but embrace adult habits, some good, some bad. We look to those who are important in our lives as role models. At almost 90 and 96, my parents are still who I turn to, and they will always be my role models. After a particularly hard night with the boys, I called Mom and Dad in tears sharing my perceived failures and the pain of parenting. They each took turns telling me that by opening my heart and home, I had made the right decision for the kids and for me. They had faith in me and wanted me to have faith in myself. I look at my siblings who are all parents and see them sharing the same Branch love we all grew up with.

#sorrymomanddad that I ever said I hated you. I didn't realize that even though it wasn't the truth, it still hurt like hell.

My boys are growing up too fast. While I can still get away with hugs and kisses at home, there's less hand holding in public. There is a magical feeling having my child's hand wrapped in mine; the skin-on-skin contact, the security they feel, and the sense of protection I feel.

#sorrymomanddad that I ever let go, seemingly embarrassed to be holding your hand as a teenager.

I make up for it now and hold their hands everywhere we go. Mostly to stop them from falling because they're 90 and 96!

My parents taught me many things growing up. The most important thing I learned as a kid was how to receive unconditional love. It's easy, you just do all the things kids do and still be loved unconditionally. The most important thing I've learned as a mom is how to give unconditional love. It's easy, you look at all the things your kids do and still love them unconditionally.

I look forward to when my sons have their own #sorrymomandmom stories. I will laugh with them the same way my folks laugh with me when I share stories of my sons.

My Sons. Sometimes it hits me out of nowhere that I'm a mom.

There's more to the story...

All my sons now share the Branch last name, and their birth certificates reflect me as Mom. In December 2020, a week after turning 97 years old, Dad took his last breath at home, surrounded by the love of family. My family continues to make sure the Branch roots that came before us continue to ripple through the memories we create for my sons' sons and daughters.

Mom has created many memories and laughs on TikTok @rootsandripples. While her heart will always ache after losing her love of almost 74 years, she smiles daily and fights to stick around. She says her goal is to outlive her great-grandmother who lived to be 106.

My sons continue to grow at warp speed. Their individual personalities shine in all they do! Their YouTube Channel, Branch Boys 6.0, has taken off slowly but they enjoy being in front of the camera sharing their thoughts, opinions, and lives as brothers.

As for me, apparently giving birth is not the only reason you have to cross your legs when you cough or sneeze. As I get older, I try to cough less to avoid crossing more.

Lana Branch

Originally from Chicago, Lana made Bloomington-Normal her home in 1986. Lana received her commission through the Illinois State University ROTC program in 1990 and her Bachelor of Arts in 2009. She is the co-founder and President/CEO of Branching Off, Inc. She and her wife own Comprehensive Health Services, a nurse staffing agency, and CHS Transport, a non-emergency wheelchair transportation company.) She has plans to open the Branch School of Health Professions to teach certified nursing courses.

Being the youngest child of a teacher and a preacher, Lana prides herself on providing educational opportunities with a cause. She teaches CPR and is a Certified Dementia Care practitioner and instructor. She is currently working to create a community-based educational program for families caring for loved ones with dementia, as well as a residential hospice house, for those in their last stages of life.

In 2014, Lana made the decision to open her heart and home to children in the foster care system and followed that through to adoption. When the knock came on February 11, 2015, two boys walked in and changed her life. There were two additional knocks on August 15, 2018, and January 17, 2019. She and her wife, Bekime, are the proud parents of Trevion, Dante, Andre, and Matthew. When not at work Lana is doing laundry (dirt plus four boys, need she say more). Becoming a mom later in life has been a challenge but is the most rewarding experience she's ever had. She can often be found on her motorcycle engaging in wind therapy.

Lana's storytelling journey has continued, and she was featured onstage in The Moth Live in October 2022.

Good Grief

By Jan Colarusso Seeley

This story was originally performed live on stage at
"That's What She Said" in Champaign, Illinois in 2015.

In October 2012, I lost my sweet husband, Joe, after his brave
21-month battle with leukemia. Joe and I were Yale classmates and
sweethearts. We moved to Champaign-Urbana in 1987 to go to grad
school at the University of Illinois, thinking we'd eventually move
back to our native New England. We never made it.

We were married 26 years, and I can honestly say they were all
pretty damn happy. We were a perfect match of kindred souls and a
great team: tall and short, quiet and loud, faster and fast. We had
common interests, shared goals, different strengths, and
unconditional love.

But Joe's untimely passing meant living the rest of my life
without him. How was I going to manage the grief that engulfed me,
ambushing me constantly, like when I would dial Joe's cell number
out of habit? The grief that pierced my heart so deeply, I had to get
a pacemaker to fix it.

As a society, we don't like to talk about grief. It is just easier to
avoid it altogether. I mean, who wants to tackle that five-ton elephant

in the room? Well, *I* am going to talk about grief, to tell you, maybe even convince you, that grief can be a good thing.

Grief has taught me that tears are good. When we cry, we purge our bodies of toxic chemicals. I read it in a book Dr. Joyce Brothers wrote after her husband died. If we don't cry, the crap doesn't have a way to get out of our bodies.

Thank you, grief.

Grief has taught me to face fire. I knew that joining the grief support group offered by a local hospice program would be brutally hard. And man, was it. Each class was like taking a firehose to the face. Becoming a "student" of grief, I learned that there is no free pass on grieving. I just had to do it. By actively choosing to grieve, I was exercising some control over an overwhelming situation.

Thank you, grief.

Grief has helped me connect more deeply to my running. Running was a huge part of my life with Joe and remains a big part of my ongoing recovery. I run to connect with Joe's spirit. On an early morning run, in the dark, with the sky full of stars and a full moon still visible overhead, I absolutely feel Joe's presence and am uplifted by it. Before he died, Joe asked me to enter specific races and to run in places that he wouldn't get to. My running has taken me to the top of Pikes Peak, the trails of Boise's Bogus Basin, and beyond. I am running more than ever and enjoying it like never before.

Thank you, grief.

Grief has helped me get over my fear of flying. The timing of Joe's death was unfortunately close to my younger son's move to college in California. Paul was joining his older brother, Jake, who was already there as a graduate student. I was going to have an empty nest, but not the empty nest I envisioned a few years earlier. I was facing a big, empty house: no Joe, no kids. Just me… and the mice.

Grief encouraged me to flip that scenario on its head, to use my new life as an opportunity to travel and to seek as much adventure as possible. Since Joe died, I have traveled to Spain, France, Czech Republic, and Finland; to California to visit my kids more times than I can count; and to run in races all over the country. This amount of travel has been a big deal for me because it involved planes, a lot of planes, and I've been a fearful flyer my entire life. To embrace this new lifestyle, I had to get over my fear of flying.

Thank you, grief.

Grief has showed me how to honor someone's memory in unique and meaningful ways. Working with the local park district, we buried Joe's remains at the base of a Majesty Sugar Maple tree planted near the large pavilion in Crystal Lake Park in Urbana and installed a handsome and sturdy memorial JOE bench near the tree.

We also honored Joe by creating a memorial fund to benefit the local soccer club that both our boys played in, and that Joe coached in for years. Through the incredible generosity of family and friends, we were able to endow the Joe fund. Since Joe coached the youngest kids in the club, through the Joe Fund, we underwrite the cost of all the uniforms for the nine-year-old boys and girls teams each fall. Joe's spirit is alive and well in Champaign-Urbana.

Thank you, grief.

Grief has taught me to lean on friends and be open to new ones. I would not be surviving without the endless love and support of my family and friends. But I have also been blessed in the time since Joe died to have some wonderful new friends come into my life, people who I believe were placed in my path because I needed them to be. I like to think Joe sent them. Thank you, Joe.

Grief has made me want to bring happiness to others. I try harder to find joy in every day and not to complain or let dumb, petty things bother me. I get immense joy from making other people happy.

As the director of the Christie Clinic Illinois Race Weekend, I am the main person who handles calls and emails from thousands of entrants. If an entrant has a question or problem, I'm their girl. My real job title, apparently, is the "make people happy person." I love this job! When I make other people happy, it makes me happy, too.

Thank you, grief.

Grief has also taught me to be more patient and to have greater faith. Joe had the patience of Job (remember: he did coach youth soccer!) Since he died, I have found the faith to believe that whatever my future is, it will unfold exactly as it was meant to be. And to be at peace with that.

Thank you, grief.

Lastly, grief has taught me to live for the moment. Giving myself over to living for the moment frees me from the pain of Joe's illness and watching him die little by little in front of my eyes.

Today, I am going to do my best to live fully. Tomorrow, I will do the same. I am mindful of enjoying all the small moments of life. "Be in the moment" is my mantra.

Thank you, grief.

The grief I've endured from losing Joe has made me a kinder, better, more empathetic person, a more thoughtful person. I am stronger and more resilient than I ever thought. I now know I can survive anything. I had these traits before Joe died. I just didn't know it the way I do now.

Thank you, grief.

Grief can make us bitter or better—I choose BETTER.
So, I will keep on living,
and cry when I need to,
and face fire every day,
and be a joyful and dedicated runner,
and seek even more travel and adventure,
and honor Joe's memory in unique ways,
and hold my family and friends dear,
and make people happy,
and be more patient,
and have more faith,
and live for the moment.

Thank you, grief.

• • •

There's more to the story...

Ten years after Joe's passing, my grief journey continues. Time has been the greatest healer, but I miss my biggest fan more with each passing day. Early morning still beckons me to the roads where I find solace. Memories of the many miles run with Joe during our 30 years together still brings me great comfort. Grief has become a kind and gentle teacher, and I am still learning every day. And helping friends who have joined the "club no one wants to join," walking beside them as they embark on their own journey.

Jan Colarusso Seeley

Jan Colarusso Seeley is a Bostonian who moved to Champaign-Urbana 35 years ago to attend graduate school at the University of Illinois. She was the publisher of Marathon & Beyond magazine for 19 years before becoming the director of the Christie Clinic Illinois Race Weekend.

A Yale graduate and former world-class field hockey player who played on the U.S. National Team, Jan turned in her stick and cleats in the early '80s and became an avid long-distance runner. Running is a constant balm for Jan, as she continues to find her way in a world that no longer includes her brave Joe, who passed away in October 2012, from leukemia, after a 21-month struggle with the disease. Jan published the blog Joe wrote during his illness as a full-length book called Joe's Blasts. She is the proud mom of two sons, Jake and Paul.

VOLUME 1

Serenity

By Genevieve Pilon

This story was originally performed live on stage at
"That's What She Said" in Bloomington, Illinois in 2019.

The first time I heard the word "lesbian," was in 1997. I was ten
years old and sitting in church, like any other Sunday. At the time,
my family attended a Southern Baptist church in the heart of the
Bible Belt, so it was fairly common to hear a sermon about hellfire
and damnation. The sermon that Sunday was more specifically about
who was going to hell, like murderers and lesbians. I leaned over in
the pew and asked my mom what a lesbian was. She told me they
were girls who liked girls.

I thought of the daydreams I frequented about rescuing pretty
damsels in distress and of the "practice" kiss I shared with the
pastor's daughter when I was eight or nine years old. *Did this mean
I liked girls?* I thought everyone did. I wasn't too worried at the time;
however, I figured that in a couple years I would go through puberty,
start liking boys, and everything would be fine.

I had enjoyed a pretty happy childhood until that point, but I
was naïve about the world. I was homeschooled through fifth grade
and my church was my only community outside of my family. In my

community, it was not even a little bit acceptable to be anything other than heterosexual. By the age of 11, I found myself unable to sleep more than an hour or two a night, if I was lucky. By the age of 12, I had hit puberty and I definitely, officially, very much liked girls. I became severely depressed and I spent my sleepless nights begging God to please make me like boys so I wouldn't go to hell.

When I started sixth grade, my family had just recently moved to Illinois, and my siblings and I began attending public school. I was awkward and shy. I preferred boyish, unfashionable clothing and I did not understand any popular culture references, as we had not had a television for a couple of years and I was not allowed to listen to mainstream music. The children I attended school with were merciless.

The bullying ranged from people competing to get food caught in my big hair to repeated sexual harassment by a group of boys. I broke down crying to a teacher the first time it happened. He sent me to the principal's office, along with the boys in question. After a short discussion, the boys were sent on their way and the principal explained to me that these things happen. The boys were just having fun. And, next time, don't make such a big deal out of it. So, I didn't. I didn't tell my parents or anyone else. It was just another secret I had to keep. I was so embarrassed; I couldn't stand the idea of talking about it again anyway.

It wasn't until near the end of seventh grade that a teacher witnessed what was happening and called the police, which ended the whole thing. My parents found out this time and decided to put me and my siblings in a private Christian school the next year. I was very excited because that's where Amy Kauffman went to school. Amy went to my church and she was beautiful. She was straight, but I had it all figured out. I would become straight, too, and we would be best friends who lived together and hugged all the time.

When I was 14, I finally came out... to my cat. She was pretty cool about it. Next, I told the neighbor boy, who was a liberal and had hinted in the past that he didn't think being gay was a big deal. His kind reaction gave me the courage to come out to my parents. My parents weren't angry, but they were as confused as I was. How could this have happened? When I told my mom, she said, "Can't you just be a nun?" I reminded her that we weren't Catholic.

THAT'S WHAT SHE SAID

The summer I turned 15, I was hospitalized for the first time for depression. After I got out, I told my youth pastor's wife and Amy the reason why I had been so sick. They decided to help me by starting a weekly Bible study for just the three of us. Every week, at the end of the Bible study, I got to hold Amy's hand when we prayed.

I was excited to go back to school my sophomore year. I had friends there and I had gotten into theater for the first time and was loving it. During my freshman year, I had been cast as the lead role in all the plays. It was a small school with only maybe 12 of us to pick from, but I was thrilled.

I knew better than to tell anyone at school my secret, but Amy had told her boyfriend. A couple of months into the school year, he told the basketball team. By the end of that week, it seemed like everyone knew. My teachers started singling out both me and my siblings and it wasn't subtle. We clearly were not welcome there, but they were happy to take our tuition.

After I was outed, the theater teacher refused to cast me in the plays as anything more than an extra, so I tried out for cheerleading and was the only girl who tried out who didn't make the team. So, instead, I threw myself into my schoolwork and I got the highest grade in my French class.

At the end of every school year there was an award ceremony and the person with the highest grade in each class would get an award. My teacher had told me I was going to get the French award. My family had decided by then to leave the school, but we still went to the ceremony. I got dressed up, and I was so excited. I waved to my French teacher when we sat in the row behind her, but she looked away without waving back. When they announced the French award, they gave it to the girl with the second highest grade, who had been disqualified the year before because she was Canadian and grew up speaking French at home.

I tried everything I could think of to get rid of these feelings and I was disgusted with myself. I prayed constantly, I studied my Bible, I learned about ex-gay groups and conversion therapy, and I was seeing a Christian counselor for his own odd variety of conversion therapy. He was actually a really nice guy, who I believe meant well, but he had no idea what he was doing. He told me I had OCD, but without the compulsive factor. He said that I was only obsessed with women, and not actually gay, because Christians can't be gay. He had me write in a journal every time I thought about a girl. Since I was a teenager, that was all the time, so I couldn't really keep up with it. But I really did try everything. So, when my friend Jennifer suggested an exorcism, I said okay.

I went over to her house on a weekend and we sat on the floor in her room. Her mom wouldn't let us use candles, so we had to keep the lights on. Jennifer warned me that she was going to speak in tongues and that it would be intense... but it was just *weird*. When she was done, I looked at a Christian boy band poster on her wall and said that maybe I felt something. But I was lying... which is a sin, by the way.

That summer, I had come to the conclusion that it would be better to be dead than gay. I spent the week of my 16th birthday in the hospital. I made friends with a couple of the girls there and I showed them how I could fit in tiny places. I would hide in the little laundry bins we had and they'd roll me up and down the hallways. They called me "roll-around Genevieve." The doctors, nurses, and the counsellors there kept telling me there was nothing wrong with being gay. I told them they were wrong. God had made some sort of mistake and God was going to help me.

I went to a new school my junior year. I don't remember much about the beginning of the year because I was very sick. I couldn't sleep and I weighed very little because I had no appetite. I thought God had forgotten me. Right before Christmas, I was hospitalized for the third and last time.

One of the days at the hospital, I was lying on the floor of my room crying. I had tried everything I could, and I was ready to give up and end my life. So, I asked God one more time to fix this terrible mistake. I asked for a sign that these feelings would go away, that I could be straight. When I was done, I felt the type of exhausted calmness I associate with a day of swimming in the sun. I dried my eyes, and I got up and walked toward the activity room at the end of the hall. When I got to the end of the hallway, I stopped and stared at the wall, because there was my sign. I must've walked by it fifty times but had never noticed it before. It said, "God, grant me the serenity to accept the things I cannot change, the courage to change the things I can, and the wisdom to know the difference."

Now, I had never read this prayer before, but I knew exactly what it meant. In my calm exhaustion, I felt something else that I can only describe as pure, unconditional love wrap around me from head to toe. With it, came the knowledge, without a doubt, that this was something I could not change. God hadn't forgotten me or made a mistake; I was whole in my creation and beautifully made.

My faith never stopped being a central part of who I am, but I left the church for a very long time. I tried a few churches over the years but there was always the fear that my welcome only went so far. Sure, in most churches I'd be welcome to walk in the door. I'd be welcome to sit in the pews and give my money and volunteer my time, but I couldn't be in a leadership position or take communion. I couldn't work with children or become a full member. I would never fully belong in a place like that.

When I was 28, I did one of the scariest things a member of the LGBTQ+ community can do, and I walked into a church I'd never been to before, alone on a Sunday morning. On the welcome table were fliers that said, "God loves people who are gay and straight, republicans and democrats, Cubs fans and Cardinals fans." It's that simple, really. It should be. I walked in that day and found a place where I was fully welcome at the table.

I have changed much from that 16-year-old who found divine wholeness in a hallway, but I don't ask God to change me anymore. I ask God to shape me into the person I should be. And I know I'm in good hands.

Genevieve Pilon

Genevieve Pilon found herself a new career as an electrician. She is passionate about traveling and living a life full of new and challenging experiences, while living as simply as possible to afford to do so. In those endeavors, she has managed to travel to over sixteen countries, has both flown a plane and jumped out of one (but not the same plane), and has recently begun strength training and weight-lifting.

Genevieve currently resides in Illinois with her cat and is very involved in her church. Her story continues to evolve, and she hopes to inspire everyone to choose love over fear each and every day.

Revenge of the World's Grossest Mom

By Leslie Marinelli

This story was originally performed live on stage at "That's What She Said" in Champaign, Illinois in 2014.

I recently overheard two of my three children playing a very rousing game of *"What's Grosser?"*

Do you know this game? The object is to gross out your opponent by pitting two disgusting scenarios against each other. For instance, "What's grosser? Finding a used Band-Aid, or someone else's hair... in your food?" It's like "Would You Rather" Junior Edition, with bonus points for making your siblings belly laugh and/or gag.

So, there I was, eavesdropping from the next room, which is usually when the most magical sibling conversations happen... and that's when I heard it:

"What's Grosser? Creamed corn? Or *Mom*?"

I was stunned. *Creamed corn? That's the best they could do? At least give me a worthy comparison like a diaper blowout.*

Of course, I put an end to that conversation immediately.

In my meanest Mom voice, "Alright, you two. Play time's over. Whose turn is it to pluck Mama's neck hair?"

(Kidding. I use my husband's nose hair trimmer for that.)

Actually though, the whole exchange got me thinking, *OMG, am I... gross?*

This called for a deeper examination. Let's review the facts: I *am* the person everyone in my house calls to determine if something is chocolate or poop. And I *have* been called "sir" by various retail clerks more times than I care to admit. But in terms of *sheer grossness*, I think the clincher was when my preteen daughter and I went bra shopping—together—*in the same fitting room.*

She was trying on these adorable little training bras which looked like two floral Band-Aids connected by a piece of string. I, on the other hand, was manually rolling each of my 32 Longs like tube socks before tucking them into what I can only describe as two canvas tote bags lined with memory foam. Yes, actual memory foam: because clearly my breasts had forgotten where they belong on my torso.

My poor daughter. She looked like a deer in the headlights. (Or in my case: floodlights.) Truly, she could not... look... away.

And then the questions started.

"When I grow up, will my nipples look like... *that?*"

Then, cringing, "Is that from breastfeeding?"

"Mom, were you ever in an industrial accident?"

After bra-shopping that day, the only thing about me more deflated than my breasts was my self-esteem.

I guess I can't blame her. It is frightening to see the effects of age, gravity, and mileage. Especially when you're young and nubile, and your nipples both face forward... and in the same direction.

Remember the Pencil Test? This was a thing my friends and I did back in the day to determine if we were ready for a real bra. Our preteen understanding was that any bare breast capable of holding up a pencil clearly needed more support than just a Frankie Say Relax t-shirt. These days I can actually hold a box of Wheat Thins under each of mine. Please don't ask how I know this.

THAT'S WHAT SHE SAID

Okay, fine. So when you add it all up, I guess I am pretty gross. But I'll have you know, I wasn't always this way. I haven't always had to dress like a traffic cone to get attention.

I think the grossness actually began with motherhood. And no, I'm not just talking about the conception.

Let's start with the labor and delivery, shall we? Listen, if it weren't for that cone-headed creature trying to claw its way down my lady luge, I never would have voluntarily evacuated my bowels on a birthing table in front of the man I love...and a roomful of medical professionals.

Sadly, daily life has gotten no less disgusting over the past 14 years. From battling head lice, to verifying that my daughter did indeed "pass" the magnet she swallowed, to successfully removing chewed bubble gum from my preschooler's genitals, this job is not for the faint of heart, or stomach.

So yes, I am gross. But you know what? I own that grossness because I have *earned* it.

I'll let you in on a little secret. I have a special little coping mechanism. And no, it's not booze…anymore. I play a little game in my head where I pretend that motherhood is like a video game. Every time I complete another disgusting task, I feel like I have unlocked another level of adventure.

What's that? Successfully extricated a Chewbacca-like hair clump from the kids' shower drain. Three stars!

Ringworm? Rotavirus? Ringworm *and* rotavirus? Pew! Pew!

Teen boy sleepover with a defcon-2 toilet clog? Bitch, please.

People, I own a 36-inch, hand-powered, commercial grade steel toilet auger I affectionately call *The Turdinator*.

Let's face it. Real life motherhood doesn't have a lot of Pinterest-worthy moments. Some days feel like they're never going to end. Other days, I can start to see the light at the end of this dark, foul-smelling tunnel.

I try not to dwell in the darkness though, because—much like that magnet my kid swallowed—this too shall pass. And based on the bounce I see in *my* mom's step, I can tell that the Grandma level of this game called Life is pretty frickin' awesome.

One day in the not-so-distant future, my daughter will be crying *to me* about her cracked and bleeding nipples as she struggles to get my precious and perfect newborn grandchild to latch on.

And God willing, I will kick my breasts out of the way and race to her side…probably with a creamed corn casserole.

• • •

There's more to the story…

I shared this story in "That's What She Said" in a dress that could stop traffic (literally – it was traffic-cone orange) and I was equally shocked and thrilled to be invited back the following year.

Unfortunately for the good people of Champaign, Illinois, I cemented my title of World's Grossest Mom in 2015 by oversharing about my excessive body hair and the time I got a Brazilian bikini wax while nine months pregnant. Suffice it to say, I was never invited back.

Story of my life!

Eight years later, I'm happy to report things are much less gross these days, but no less exciting. As my three children have gotten older, the expression "little kids, little problems; big kids, big problems" comes to mind.

Earlier this year, my 19-year-old fell off the top of an actual waterfall and miraculously survived a harrowing seven-hour rescue operation. (Why yes, it was indeed the same kid who brought home lice, swallowed a magnet, and had a piece of chewed bubblegum stuck to her genitalia… how did you guess?)

This much I know: there is nothing quite like a child's near-death experience to put all those gross motherhood moments into perspective. What I wouldn't give for the days when my biggest challenge was a rampant case of interspecies ringworm.

Maybe having the World's Grossest Mom isn't the worst thing though. My kids have proven time and again they're resilient and resourceful as hell. All three of them know how to successfully remove at least a dozen different kinds of stains, perform the Heimlich maneuver, and auger a toilet.

My oldest son is an Eagle Scout and a recent college graduate, but what I appreciate the most about him is his brilliant sense of humor and ability to stay calm in a crisis. When our septic tank backed up several years ago and flooded two stories of my home, he created a crime scene board to solve the mystery of who caused the disaster and titled it: "Poo Done It?" I've never been prouder.

My youngest son is a sophomore in high school and loves being an only child for the first time. He's a pole vaulter, which takes way more courage in my opinion than getting onstage to tell more than a thousand people about my 32 Longs. He speaks mostly in grunts these days, but the one full sentence he says every morning on his way out the door is always "I love you, Mom."

And the other two wonder why he's my favorite! (I'm just kidding, other two. I dislike you all the same.)

The middle child, my only daughter, whose ringtone on my phone is now "Don't Go Chasin' Waterfalls," continues to keep me on my toes plotting sweet grandmotherly revenge. I credit her with every gray hair on my head, which she says looks amazing on me. Yes, can you believe it? Former Miss Nipple Shamer has evolved into a beacon of body positivity. I can't get enough of her.

My husband and I celebrated our 25th wedding anniversary this year. I may be grosser than creamed corn, but I must be doing something right.

Leslie Marinelli

Leslie Marinelli started blogging for fun in 2008 to feel like less of an invisible vessel for children and PTA donations. Her humor writing hobby morphed into a full-time job as the Editor-in-Chief and eventually the CEO of InThePowderRoom.com, an international women's humor webzine. Leslie has been featured in *The Huffington Post, CNN's Headline News, Parenting Magazine*, and *Northside Woman*. She has been named an Erma Bombeck Writers' Workshop Humorist of the Month, a BlogHer Humor Voice of the Year (twice), a Babble Top 100 Mom Blogger, and the Best Story Writer of her second grade class. She was even on Oprah once, but it was an episode about hoarding, so her family thinks she should stop bragging about it. She is the editor and co-author of the best-selling women's humor anthology, *"You Have Lipstick on Your Teeth."* Originally from Pittsburgh, Pennsylvania, Leslie has spent the last five years working for a public library system in Georgia, first as a children's librarian, and currently as a communications manager. Connect with her at LeslieMarinelli.com.

Walking Through the Valley

Jennifer Hays Schottland

This story was originally performed live on stage at "That's What She Said" in Champaign, Illinois in 2014.

My sister, Tricia Evans, was an ordinary woman who got an extraordinary disease, and she let it make her...extraordinary.

Four years ago, at the age of 40, Tricia started limping. Four months later, she was diagnosed with ALS, amyotrophic lateral sclerosis, Lou Gehrig's Disease. ALS is the gradual loss of muscle control. Prognosis is three to five years. She was not an athlete, and it does not run in our family. She was no more likely to get it than you or me.

Tricia had always been healthy growing up, rarely getting sick and often having perfect attendance in school, as well as typically getting straight A's. Tricia was my older sister; we were three years apart. Growing up, it didn't seem like we had very much in common. She was the neat, punctual go-getter. I was the messy, always late, lazy one. Most of my childhood memories with Tricia include her bossing me around and saying mean things to me, like "don't cry,

73

baby." Which, of course, almost always made me cry. And which she thought was freaking hilarious.

As we got older, we grew closer. I was maid of honor in her wedding. She was matron of honor in both of my weddings. We tried to always be there for each other, coming to the hospital when both of our two daughters were born, and attending most of the baptisms, birthday parties, etc. But we didn't make it to all of them. She was busy, I was busy. We had our own lives and they rarely intersected, except during the holidays. And even then, we couldn't be around each other more than a couple of hours before easing back to bossy big sister and annoying little sister roles.

When Tricia turned 40, she was living her best life. She had just re-entered the workforce as a special education teacher. She had taken time off to be a stay-at-home mom to her beautiful daughters, Kelly and Sarah. They were ages six and eleven, both in school full-time. She was active in her church, the local Down syndrome network, and she had an active social life that included a couple of nights a month of her favorite activity: karaoke. And she was really good at it, too. Not that she was an amazing singer, she could carry a tune good enough, but she would just have so much fun. Her enthusiasm was contagious!

The timing of her illness and diagnosis were devastating. She was so young. Her kids were so young. We had a couple of grandparents still alive. Our family had never gone through a tragedy like this before. How could we cope?

Throughout her journey, Tricia used the internet to send updates to her family and friends. I would like to share a few of her posts with you.

March 2013

First a quick summary of the past year. Breathing became difficult so Jim [Tricia's husband] *and I made the decision to prolong my time with my family with the help of a ventilator. I was able to be at home on the vent thanks to my amazing friends, nurses, and family. During this time, I gradually lost the ability to swallow, speak, and the thing I'm missing most right now, the ability to smile. This past fall I made the move to Prairie Rose* [nursing home]. *A year ago, like anyone, I was thinking NO WAY would I go to a nursing home, but here I am and I am here by my own choice. Everyone asks me how do I get through it. This disease is unimaginable, but it's not like it happened overnight. Each loss was gradual and gave me time to mourn and adjust. Meanwhile I got to witness the awesome, fantabulous people in our lives.*

She sounds pretty upbeat, right? What she doesn't mention, is that the nursing home was 90 minutes away from home. She also doesn't mention how difficult it is for her to communicate. She used her eyes to communicate as they were about the only part of her body she had any control over by this point. We used an alphabet board so she could spell out her words to us. She would look to the right for "yes" and to the left for "no."

Imagine your mind as a bucket, and your thoughts as water in the bucket. Most of us can pour out our thoughts quickly. Tricia was only able to dispense her thoughts out one drop at a time, one letter at time, without tone and voice inflection, facial expressions, or body language. It was difficult to know when she was joking or being sarcastic. She still had her sense of humor, but she could still be a bitch. (I said she was extraordinary, not perfect!)

A couple months later, in May 2013, Tricia recorded these thoughts:
A while ago, someone read me a devotional about waiting, hoping, and trusting. As you can imagine, I do a lot of waiting. I wait each week for Sunday, the day Jim and the girls [her daughters, ages 8 and 13 at the time] *come. I'm also waiting to die. It could be today, next month, or five years from now. I wish I knew. Do I even want to live like this? Heaven sounds like a pretty nice place. I'm hoping Kelly and Sarah are doing OK without me. I'm hoping Jim is not too stressed. I'm hoping for a miracle. I want to walk out of here – go back to being a mom. I'm trusting God to take care of my family. Somehow, He has a plan, and I will trust Him with my life.*

A few months later, she wrote about her not so good days:
Some days I feel so sad, like "how can I put up with all of this shit for one more day?" So I ask for an ativan and listen to my music and cry. But some days I find myself thinking, "I love this place, it feels like a big family!" [The staff took amazing care

of her.] *The difference between these two feelings all comes down to peace. Peace to me means faith... giving up control and not worrying.*

In November, Tricia was able to go home for a weekend. *My favorite place is home. Going home is quite an ordeal. But it's all worth it! I always wanted a house that was newer and bigger, with nicer furniture and no clutter* [sound familiar?] - *but none of that matters to me anymore. I've learned that JOY doesn't come from "things." The best parts were Sarah dancing, Kelly playing her clarinet, and Jim playing his guitar and singing a song he just wrote for me. These are all things I used to take for granted.*

Peace and joy. Tricia figured out that gratitude - being thankful for what you do have - brings trust and hope. And that trust and hope bring peace and joy. Yeah, I want that, too. So, if I think about all of the things I'm thankful for, I'll realize how abundantly blessed I am. Because of that, I can trust that everything is going to be okay. I can have hope for my future. And that brings me peace and joy.

Seven months after Tricia was able to go home for a weekend, she decided it was time to go home forever. To her heavenly home. She had begun losing control of her eyes and did not want to be "locked-in," completely unable to communicate. It was time, she decided, to have the ventilator turned off. June 4th, 2014. Eleven days before her 44th birthday. She got excited to go to heaven. She trusted that her family would be okay. She never wanted to give up, but because of her peace and joy, was ready to let go.

Our lives are full of mountains and valleys, one moment we're on top of the world, and the next we feel we've hit rock bottom. I always want to remember when I'm walking through a valley to not let my circumstances be a slide down to a deep, dark pit of despair, but rather steppingstones to the mountain tops of hope and joy. I want to let my extraordinary circumstances make me extraordinary.

Jennifer Hays Schottland

Jennifer Hays Schottland, MSW, is a school social worker, wife, daughter, and mother of two teenagers. She is passionate about her faith, serving others, and protecting our planet. Although a soft-spoken introvert, Jen loves people and strives to inspire hope and joy. In her spare time, Jen likes to hang out and play games with family and friends.

VOLUME 1

Soggy Teddy Bear

By Isak Griffiths

This story was originally performed live on stage at "That's What She Said" in Champaign, Illinois in 2015.

I was a beautiful, arms-wide-open, happy, happy child. When I was seventeen months old, my mother still had to prop me up on the couch with pillows tucked in all around me so that I wouldn't roll off and couldn't fall down. I would sit there all day, every day, singing to myself, chattering with anyone who would come by, happy as could be. Later, my mom could stand me up on a stool with a bottle of Windex and a full roll of paper towels, and I would clean a single window singing and chattering to myself for hours, perfectly content.

Then, in the middle of one night, I woke up screaming from a horrible, horrible nightmare. Shaking. Terrified. Crying. And you moms know that a child who is stubborn can scream and cry for a long, long, long time. But no one came to comfort me.

I was three years old.

So, in my little flannel footed pajamas, now holding a very soggy teddy bear, I padded to my mom's bedroom. But the door was closed. In fact, it was locked, and I didn't even know my mom's room had a lock. For a moment, I thought something was really, really wrong. Crying, I pounded on the door and I called out to my mom. But she didn't answer. I didn't know what else to do. So, I kicked. And I called out. But my mom didn't answer.

Eventually, I realized that there were voices on the other side of the door. At first there were whispers. Then, there were shouting whispers, and then there were sobs. And then, there was more.

My father was there. In my memory, at the time, my father was a shadowy figure who would appear from time to time. And, in some ways, he was my hero. He'd let me sit on his foot as he walked around the apartment. Or he'd take me with him when he'd go out, and he'd set me up on a bar in a bar eating pig skins with hot sauce and sipping beer. But he was also a man that frightened me.

So, in the moment, outside that door, I calmed myself down, and I listened. I could hear my mom begging and pleading to get to me. I heard her crying and sobbing. I heard her clawing and fighting to get to me. And I heard my father fighting back.

He was hurting my mom. Because I was outside that door crying. He was hurting her because I was scared. He was hurting my mom because I needed her. And since that night, I have never been the same.

That night, I learned that if someone cared about me, they would suffer, and they would feel pain. I learned that no matter how hurt and scared I was, no one would be there for me. Not even my mom. I learned that no matter how hurt and how scared I got, I should feel terribly, terribly alone because, if I asked you to be there for me, I'd be asking you to be hurt and scared. And when you got injured, it would be all my fault.

All my life, I waited for a fairy tale mother who would appear, wave her magic wand, and make my life easy. I wanted a mom who could kiss my bruises and make all the pain go away. But that fairy tale mom never came. Instead, for years, I cried. I spit. I kicked. I fought. I pounded and I screamed, waiting for my life to get better. And it didn't.

Eventually, thanks to the help of an incredible therapist, I came to accept how much I hated feeling so angry and so hurt and so abandoned all... the... time. More importantly, I came to understand that I would never, ever change my past. But that I could change me.

I will always be at my core a frightened little girl in flannel footed pajamas holding on tight to a soggy teddy bear. To deny this would be a lie.

But that reality is incomplete. I think... I think reality can be revised; I think... I think it can be improvised. So, now every day that I'm alive, I choose laughter. I choose joy. And I choose love. I choose to listen and to care and to trust. And I choose to be someone that I genuinely like. These are not hats that I put on or faces that I wear. In truth, sometimes I choose better than others because I am a work in progress. But I am reclaiming that eyes-wide-open, happy, happy child.

At times, I still love to sing. And at times, I still love to chatter. Still, sometimes, to this day, I feel terribly, terribly alone. But it doesn't mean that I am, and it doesn't mean that I have to be.

In truth, I am surrounded by women who are in part, like me — little girls holding on to soggy teddy bears... Intelligent, kind, courageous women... Beautiful, strong, and compassionate women.

Trust me. Flannel footed pajamas or no, you are not and you, too, never have to be alone.

Choose. Please choose. Because your reality is up to you.

• • •

There's more to the story...

When Jenette and Kerry invited me to join "That's What She Said" in 2015, their specific ask of me was to tell the one story I had never told anyone before. I accepted their challenge, but I was unprepared for the shattering vulnerability I would feel opening up that still-wounded part of me to the world. Since then, I have met so many women who held similar moments silently inside until my story touched their hearts. It's these conversations that helped me find words to describe how I began to heal, and it's these words that became my first book, *Child of God: You are Already Perfect.* The little girl in this story will always be a part of me. Please know that I love her deeply — soggy teddy bear and all.

Isak Griffiths

Her name, which sounds like eeSOCK, means "she laughs." It's a perfect name for a woman who values laughter, inclusion, celebration, and a sense of freedom. Isak knows that while life is often unkind and unfair, she has learned that there is no joy in choosing the pain and stagnation of living in the past. She is an executive coach who encourages people to see challenges as opportunities, and to always embrace learning something new. Following her own advice, she has studied Japanese swordsmanship in Kyoto and drumming in Guinea, worked on business-building with women in India and Tanzania, and taught people how to ride motorcycles. Isak is a wife, a mother, and an Orthodox Christian. She is an author, artist, musician, and inspiring speaker. But mostly, Isak is exactly what she challenges and invites others to be: fully human. Connect with Isak at honestimpact.com.

VOLUME 1

RIP Donna Martin

By Heidi Cordes

This story was originally performed live on stage at "That's What She Said" in Champaign, Illinois in 2019.

The year was 2009, and we were headed to the Kentucky Derby. For any of you that have been to the Kentucky Derby, you know that the women get *dressed*. These women are thinking about their outfit or their style for the entire year. My best friend Colleen - my "bestie" - and I did the same thing. For an entire year, we planned our dresses, our hats, our jewelry, our makeup, our bags, everything you could think of. We spent a whole year putting it together.

Leading up to the Derby, Colleen and I paid attention to all the celebrity action. We made a mental list of the celebrities rumored to be attending. That year, some of the celebs attending were Usher, Tara Reid, Tori Spelling, Jamie Lynn Sigler, and a ton of notable athletes, to name a few.

We also had very good seats, thanks to Colleen. She knew someone who knew someone, so we were one level beneath

Millionaires Row where all of the *top* celebs would be; we were thrilled!

We had a little pregame at the house, just a drink or two before our big day, and we arrived at Churchill Downs around 9:00 a.m. We walked through the paddock, found our seats, hit the bar, and ordered our "ceremonial" Mint Juleps. We order Mint Juleps because they are a Derby tradition, not because they taste any good. Our second drink is always the lovely Lily, another traditional Derby drink. That drink actually tastes great and helps wash down all of the bourbon from the Mint Julep. The actual Kentucky Derby race was the 10th race of the day, so we had all day to enjoy lots and lots of Lilies.

There is another sport that goes on at Churchill Downs on the first Saturday in May. There is not just horse racing, there is also the sport of "Lady Watching." I spend all day admiring other women's styles, their hats, their dresses, their bags, how they put their outfits together. What does their makeup look like? What vibe are they going for?

I am 90% consumed with Lady Watching and only about 10% interested in the race. Lady Watching is a sport. I am a professional. I am the G.O.A.T. (Greatest Of All Time).

We were congregating near the bar and the betting windows, standing and chatting with our husbands and friends. I had one eye in the conversation talking to everyone, and one eye roaming the room. I positioned myself so I can see the escalator that comes down from Millionaires Row because I was there to do some serious Lady and Celeb Watching like it is my job.

Someone who knows someone brought Steve Young over to chat with us… Steve Young. NFL Hall of Fame quarterback, Steve Young. He's 6'2", 215 lbs., with a great head of hair. He was very friendly and chatty, but he is *just* a football player. As we were all talking, my left eye locked on the escalator, and I. Saw. Her. *My* celebrity. Floating like a goddess down the escalator was *Tori Spelling.* TORI SPELLING!

The moment I'd been waiting for had arrived… and it was GO TIME. So, I bull-rushed Steve Young like a 320 lb. defensive lineman with 0% body fat. I was using my swim moves to get him out of my way going as fast as I could, while yelling "Tori! Tori Spelling! Tori!"

We were not that far away. She could hear me. There is no doubt she could hear me, but she was laser focused on making her exit.

Finally, it became clear to me that she is not going to look my way, nor is she even going to acknowledge me. She was moving through the crowd, as I am hustle-walking to reach her, but I couldn't run. Let's be real: I was in heels and my boobs were taped into my dress. If I ran, I would have tripped, broken an ankle and my boobs would be flying everywhere. This story would be about ambulances and boobies flying everywhere, instead of telling you all about the day I was destined to become best friends with Tori Spelling.

So, as I'm still trying to get to her, calling "Tori! Tori!" I heard from a distance, coming in fast, my wingman, Colleen. I hear her calling "Donna Martin! Donna Martin!" Colleen and I are converging as we shuffle our way to befriend Tori Spelling, a.k.a. Donna Martin from *Beverly Hills 90210*.

But for some strange reason, she *refused* to look at us; she just kept walking toward the exit. We finally realized that she is not going to give us the time of day.

We stood there completely confused.

"Are you serious?"

"She didn't even turn her head."

Colleen and I considered the blatant snub: it's not like she was the biggest celebrity at that moment. I mean, this was post-90210, pre-comeback, pre-reality show. She was not even an "A-list" celebrity. She was more like a "G." *That's* the level of her celebrity and she couldn't even look at us.

Obviously, she doesn't know that Colleen and I are pretty amazing. We are smart, savvy, strong, independent women. We know how to live our very best lives. We bring the party. We would have been very good for Tori Spelling. We could have been there for her. She was *our* celebrity. We were totally prepared and ready to guide her through life and be *best* friends.

Bitch didn't look at us once.

Did not tilt her head.

Did not turn her neck.

She did not even give us a side eye.

She totally dismissed us.

She is now dead to us.

RIP DONNA MARTIN!

We get back to business and keep on drinking. The jokes were flying for the rest of the day. We love a good joke. And if *we* are the joke, that's even better. We just enjoyed our moment of getting blown off by an "L-list" celebrity. We had such a good laugh and now we're going to have this story to remember forever.

Before the actual Derby race started, I needed to make a trip to the restroom. Now, we were on one of the higher levels and they had really nice restrooms. They have an *attendant*. There're only two stalls and the doors go all the way from top to bottom, from ceiling to floor. So, you can't see underneath, because you know I'd be down on all fours staring at shoes the whole time. But I was there in line waiting, and at this point I was like 65-70% in the tank and standing still is not as easy as it was when we arrived at Churchill Downs, so I'm leaning on the wall for support. But I didn't want to look like I was leaning on the wall, because this is the Derby and I want to look classier than the average girl at a club. So, I tenderly leaned against the wall, careful to keep my hat and sunglasses in place, as part of my complete look, of course.

There were two girls in line behind me who looked like supermodels, and I heard them whispering. I thought to myself, *seriously, are they freaking talking about how drunk I am?* So, I leaned back a little bit more dangerously to hear what they were saying, and I heard them say, "Meadow Soprano is in here."

Without missing a beat, I thought to myself, *RIP Tori Spelling, Meadow Soprano's in here! When she comes out of that stall, I'm going to make small talk, and we're going to chat it up.* She's *going to be our new best friend. And then Colleen and I are going to be able to guide* her *through life.* I had a new plan.

I turned around to the girls and I asked, "Did you say Meadow Soprano is in here?" And this beautiful model looked at me – looked *down* at me...she's six feet tall and all legs. This beautiful model looked down at me and said with pure disgust, "Eww...we thought it was *you!*"

I nearly peed my dress right there for two reasons. The first was that someone thought *I* was Meadow Soprano. The second was because when I turned around, I ruined *their* celebrity moment. I have to be honest, that made me feel so much better.

Heidi Cordes

Heidi Cordes grew up in East Moline, Illinois and has spent her adult life in Central Illinois. She is the proud mom to her son, Jackson, and enjoys watching him pursue his dreams. She is a people person who never lets her circumstances define her. When she was diagnosed with Lupus in 2009, she immediately became an expert and an advocate to those with this unique condition. When asked to speak in "That's What She Said," she was challenged to find her story, without talking about Lupus. By making the choice that she is "more than her diagnosis," Heidi instead chose to share one of the funniest things that has ever happened to her. Since that night, she has embraced the healing power of laughter and asks her friends to share their hilarious stories. She spends her free time volunteering, bonding with her family, and occasionally pursuing celebrities.

VOLUME 1

Trust Your Journey

By Karyl Wackerlin

This story was originally performed live on stage at
"That's What She Said" in Champaign, Illinois in 2015.

One month ago tonight, I was sitting around a campfire in Haiti,
making s'mores with the kids at God's Littlest Angels Orphanage
and the 10 passionate women who had made the trip to Haiti with
me.

As coordinator of Soul Journey, one of my goals is to design
trips that empower, encourage, and inspire not only the women on
our teams, but the GLA staff and Haitian women we meet along the
way.

It takes passion and a sense of purpose to put these trips
together, but before I could start, I had to go on a Soul Journey of
my own.

Mine began on August 27, 2007 – I remember that day like it
was yesterday.

VOLUME 1

We had just left home for a job interview in Atlanta. It was 10 a.m. – way too early in the day for my husband to be slurring his words as he talked on the phone. I didn't need more proof that he'd already been drinking that morning, and with an uncanny sense of calm, I closed my eyes, said a prayer, and asked him to take me home.

I was ready to make the decision that life on my own would be better than life in the chaos that had taken over our 36-year marriage.

In the quiet of the car that morning, the decision seemed easy to make, but the months that led up to that decision had *not* been so simple. In trying to make sense of life in a home controlled by alcohol, I had become bitter, angry, and resentful. I'd perfected the art of walking on eggshells, and my self-esteem and dreams had gone down the tubes.

Memories of all our good years faded as I became consumed with the pain of the last few. I became a master at pretending that everything was "just fine" while, secretly, I felt like our marriage was spinning out of control. I literally lost my voice and reached out to food, family, and friends for the comfort I wasn't getting at home.

I was sucking the life out of my closest friendships as I bored my friends with detail after detail of my life as a victim. Though they were sympathetic, I'm sure my best friends were thankful for Caller ID!

During those years, I learned that there are many ways to numb the pain. I would never have used alcohol. You see, my grandfather was an alcoholic, and I'd heard many stories about my grandfather's late-night binges and the effect they had on my mother and her family.

But I discovered my own way to numb the pain – eating a lot, traveling and working a lot, and even getting overly involved in church work. I craved attention and tried to control whatever, and whoever, I could.

What I realize now, is that while I was numbing the pain, I was also numbing the joy.

On that August morning in 2007, when I knew that life as I knew it was over, what I didn't realize is that it had just begun.

God had not only given me the courage to say, "I'm done," but the compassion to see the pain my husband was in, and the willingness to help him find a residential treatment program when he said he was ready to get help.

I finally realized that the choice to stay or leave was mine, and I chose to stay.

And then, I began a slow journey back to joy.

I began to focus on myself. Instead of telling friends I was "just fine," I learned to be specific about what I needed – chocolate and Chipotle. On the days when I was too exhausted to get dressed, my friends would arrive at my door and would refuse to leave until I got dressed and joined them for a walk around the block.

Friends and family prayed for me, took me to Alanon meetings so I didn't have to go alone, and even took me to the Riverboat to mindlessly feed the slots.

Our kids were grown and living out of town. One called daily, just to check in; the other was supportive but more distant, and sent daily letters of encouragement to her father.

I wish I could tell you that I wrote letters, too, but I didn't. He received many letters from family and friends while he was in rehab, but not one of them was from me. I'm not proud of that, but I trust it was part of my journey – learning how to detach.

After 28 days in rehab, my husband's counselor called to say he was ready to come home.

"Home? Are you kidding me? I'm not ready for him to come home yet!"

Not much had changed except geography – he was in Minnesota and I was in Champaign. I was seeing a counselor, but spent most of my time talking about him and his drinking.

Those first few months after rehab were hard as we navigated a new world for both of us, learning to set new boundaries and "stay in our own lanes."

Our counselors told us to mind our own business – he should work on his recovery and I should work on mine, but that we needed to find a way to share space without talking about our issues. So, what did we do? Together, we watched three full seasons of "24."

I'll forever be grateful to Jack Bauer for providing us with drama that didn't include us!

I'd be lying if I said it was fast or easy. It took many months until I felt things really begin to change and it had nothing to do with Gary, and everything to do with me.

On the journey back to joy, I had to learn to forgive and put resentments behind me. I had to learn about the disease of alcoholism and the effect it had on each of us, to learn how to give up my victim role, and how to accept responsibility for the ways I had contributed to the chaos in our home.

Now, eight years later, I can say that I'm proud of the work we've put into ourselves and our marriage. On August 27 of this year, just two months after our 44th wedding anniversary, Gary celebrated eight years of sobriety. He now leads a ministry for others struggling with hurts, habits, and hang-ups. I lead the women's recovery group, and have just returned from my third Soul Journey to Haiti.

As I packed for this Haiti trip, I was amazed to see how much I could fit into my backpack. Eight years ago, I was lugging around so much dead weight that there was no room for the joy or the cameras I use to see the world. Back then, my backpack was loaded down with resentments, anger, hurts from my childhood, need for approval, low self-esteem, and pride. Some of those burdens I'd put there myself, and some were added by family members and others. It's incredible to see how much lighter my load became when I got rid of all that dead weight. These days, I pack light, free of the hurts of the past, with a keen sense of purpose and joy.

I love to see how God has used every detail of my life – the pain of those years of chaos, my years as a photographer, my friendships in this community, everything – in creating a new purpose for my life. I am confident that had it not been for the pain, I would not have experienced the joy.

When I left for Haiti last month, a friend surprised me with a bracelet that read:

For every woman who has struggled, questioned, realized, believed, accomplished, and triumphed... TRUST YOUR JOURNEY

I am that woman. I have finally learned to trust my journey. My soul and my home are filled with joy again.

• • •

There's more to the story...

So much has happened since that day in 2007. In 2021, we celebrated our 50th wedding anniversary, surrounded by family and friends, old and new. Both of our children are now married, and we have seven active grandkids who are being raised to trust God with their *own* journeys.

In 2018, we left the city in Illinois where we'd lived for almost 50 years to start retirement life in a strange new place, with no church, no friends, and no jobs. Scary, yes, but we'd actually done that before – on that day in August of 2007, when we left all that was familiar and ventured into a new way of life. What we knew with certainty *this* time, was that God was already there, preparing a place for us. He had been faithful years ago, preparing the way for our new adventure, equipping us for new ministries, promising to be with us when times got tough, or lonely, or overwhelming, so we could enter this new phase of our life with an uncanny sense of calm. With His help, I will continue to Trust the Journey.

Karyl Wackerlin

A self-professed emotion and beauty junkie, Karyl has traveled worldwide with her cameras, capturing images that touch the soul. As a professional photographer for 40 years, Karyl has used her cameras to capture the emotions of each stage of life, but her true passion is for humanitarian photography. She has traveled across the globe to photograph young patients awaiting much-needed cleft lip surgery in the Philippines, teach photography in a tiny village in Malawi, capture the emotions of children in orphanages in Peru, Mexico, and Haiti, and record the devastation in New Orleans after Hurricane Katrina. In 2014, she founded She Said's Soul Journey and led five teams of women on mission trips to a hilltop orphanage in Haiti. Soul Journey's purpose was to empower, encourage, and inspire not only the women on the teams, but the orphanage staff and other Haitian women they encountered along the way. Karyl is the mother of two and grandmother of seven, and lives with her husband, Gary, in Griffin, Georgia.

I Am Somebody

By Arlene Hosea

This story was originally performed live on stage at "That's What She Said" in Bloomington, Illinois in 2021.

My maternal grandmother, Hattie Pearl Reed Moore, would stand tall, spread her feet apart, firmly place her hands on her hips and say, "I am Hattie Moore, I am somebody."

She was born on March 28, 1909, in Crystal Springs, Mississippi, in what was a much different time than I was born into in 1959. I can only imagine what life was like during her childhood and young adult years in Mississippi before she came up north. My Mawma was a proud, hardworking, accomplished Christian woman. She would sit us down, often, and remind us why we had to believe, no matter what, that we were somebody, too.

I didn't know at the time why this was important to her or how she learned this, or what life in the early 1900's in Mississippi had put her through. But it was a lesson I carried with me, and found that I've had to draw on this lesson when faced with situations, with people, who would try to knock me down.

Let me tell you about my retirement celebration on December 2, 2014. My 25-year career at the institution was concluding. I had

97

started as an assistant manager back in 1990 and was retiring as director of one of the largest service departments on campus. I like to say that I grew up at the university because I would attend football games as a young girl to see my future brother-in-law, Walt, on the field. It was a beloved place for me.

The master of ceremony for the celebration was introducing the next speaker on the agenda. The speaker was my immediate supervisor, and it was his time to say a few words about me and my career at the university. I had worked with him for over 13 years and directly reported to him for the last four. Historically, when someone is retiring from the institution, this is a time for supervisors to talk about the retirees' career highlights, their contributions, awards, or recognition they have achieved. These events usually involve the retiree's family, members from community, colleagues, and co-workers, and were handled as gracious affairs.

This event was not just special for me because I was retiring, but because my 87-year-old mother was in attendance. That was a huge deal for me. My mother never saw me run track or cheer during junior high and high school. She never saw me compete as a member of my high school speech team, she was not present when I was introduced as a member of my high school homecoming court, and she never saw me act in To Kill A Mockingbird. No, she missed so many of my events because of health reasons, but she was present that day.

The location was special too, because it was in the same building where my parents and grandparents watched me walk across the stage to receive my bachelor's degree in 1982 and my hooding ceremony for my master's degree in 1984. This day was even more special because it would be the only retirement reception she would ever attend for any of her 10 children. I was very happy to have her there, along with so many family and friends; the room was full.

Now, my supervisor is at the microphone, and it goes something like this, "During lunch I needed to work on what I would say today. I looked in Arlene's file and it was empty, nothing there. So, I decided to Google her name, and there was a lot there." I would like to note, that as a supervisor, we kept a folder for each employee, where copies of previous evaluations are kept, copies of discipline letters, notes about good or bad things, awards, recognition, etc. Mine was empty, he said.

A bit later he was saying something about me that he found via Google and referred to me as a "he". Some people in the audience yelled out "She! She's a *she!*" He let us know that he had gotten some peanut butter and jelly smeared on the paper since he was composing this during his lunch time.

As he was speaking, I thought about our one-on-ones over the years when I spoke about my family or about being on several boards for non-profits in the community. We discussed how my leadership team and I, along with student leaders, had developed a plan to overhaul the campus dining meal plans, led multi-million dollar major renovations of two residential dining centers, and helped develop and acquire new dining concepts in the student center. But none of that was shared, as I recall. I also served on several committees for student affairs and other areas of campus, but I do not recall hearing those details about my career accomplishments. Perhaps I was in shock and bewildered after hearing that my employee file was empty and that he wrote his comments while chowing down on a peanut butter and jelly sandwich during his lunch break.

In spite of his disregard for me, I was very happy there were three speakers that day who did talk about me and shared my accomplishments. I owe so much gratitude to Terri, Linda, and Pat. I guess I should not have expected more from this person who once told me I was an "embarrassment to the university" after I followed *his* direct orders and carried out *his* plan, while he was on vacation in the Greek Isles.

In that moment, I knew I had a choice. I could let the anger and disgust well up inside me and ruin my party. Or I could ignore it and pretend I wasn't insulted by Dr. PB&J's lack of respect or decency. I could let this man make me believe that I wasn't worthy of a proper speech, that my 25 years of hard work and contribution didn't matter. Or, I could see that God puts people in your life for a reason, even horrible bosses, to help you find your strength to believe in yourself.

And then I remembered my Mawma, because for a significant portion of her life, society in America told her and treated her as though she was not somebody important and worthy. Maybe she found her inspiration in the poem written by Reverend William

Holmes Borders, Sr., "I AM Somebody," and she would stand in front of her grandchildren, with her hands on her hips and recite loudly, "I AM Somebody."

Well, I enjoyed the rest of my retirement party. I let my friends and family celebrate me and my accomplishments. And most importantly, I made my Mama proud.

Whenever I feel like the world is setting me up to fail, I stand tall, spread my feet apart, place my hands on my hips and say, "I am Arlene Hosea, I AM Somebody."

Arlene Hosea

Arlene is the ninth child and seventh daughter of ten children born to Lawrence and Josephine Mazique Hosea in Bloomington, Illinois. She was raised and educated in Bloomington and was blessed to have grown up with her paternal and maternal grandparents, who had a significant role in her upbringing. Her grandmothers were excellent cooks and passed the love of food and cooking to her. Arlene likes to share that her grandmothers cooked "soul food, food made with love." Now retired after a 30-year career in university and healthcare food service management, she resides in Normal, Illinois and is serving her second term as a Trustee for Normal Township, volunteers with several non-profits, and spends as much time as possible with her grandchildren.

VOLUME 1

There's more to the story...

Each of the women in this book originally developed their story for a stage performance of "That's What She Said."

These performances, and all stories shared on the She Said stage, can be viewed in our video archive on YouTube.

We invite you to enjoy the original performances of these sixteen stories and get to know the women behind the stories.

If you are seeking more ways to enjoy stories and conversations with some extraordinary women, check out The She Said Project Podcast wherever you find your podcasts.

VOLUME 1

THE SHE SAID PROJECT

What started as a one-night, live storytelling event in Champaign, IL, has grown into a community of women supporting women through the power of storytelling. We believe all women have a seat at the table and deserve to be heard.

Considered the "mothership" of our shows and programs, The She Said Project is our platform for sharing women's stories. We are building a community that makes accessibility and diversity a priority, and we strive to represent as many voices as possible.

The mainstage event, "That's What She Said," can be found in numerous cities and growing. The She Said Project licenses the rights to produce "That's What She Said" and provides training for new producers. The She Said Project Podcast was developed in partnership with Illinois Public Media and is hosted by Jenette Jurczyk and Kerry Rossow. Each episode welcomes a woman who has appeared onstage at "That's What She Said," and allows their story to be experienced by an even greater audience. You can find the podcast at NPR.org or wherever you listen to your favorite podcasts.

We are constantly looking at ideas, old and new, considering ways to expand our mission. With so many amazing and impactful stories shared to date, we are often asked what's next? So many women we meet want to dive deeper into sharing their own stories. We felt compelled to launch the She Said Press to publish our own collections of stories, as well as women's memoirs.

Learn more about what we are doing at shesaidproject.com

THAT'S WHAT TEENS SAY

We are super proud of our teen empowerment program, "That's What Teens Say," designed to give teens the confidence to find their voice and share their story.

When we first launched a weekend program, where teen girls were asked to give up their phones for three days in exchange for spending quality time with caring mentors, we didn't know what to expect. We quickly learned that as soon as we gave them permission to explore topics that were important to them, all we had to do was sit back and listen.

We have witnessed girls push the very edges of their comfort zones as they stand boldly and bravely on a stage and share a story from their life's experience. We have been blown away as girls shared stories about such topics as anxiety, depression, body image, bullying, coming out, disabilities, toxic relationships and more. We have seen the pride, joy and tears on their faces as their words move the audience to applause. We know this is an experience that will stay with them for a lifetime.

This three-day curriculum is available for organizations looking for quality teen programming.

To empower as many teen girls as possible, proceeds from the sale of this book will go to support the growth of this important program.

Learn more at thatswhatteensay.com

ABOUT THE "PRODUCER"

Jenette Jurczyk wakes up every morning still wondering how this is her life. As the National Director of The She Said Project, Jenette is the driving force behind the growth of the organization and the expansion of "That's What She Said" into new communities.

Jenette started directing the live shows in 2015 and has never looked back. Now with dozens of shows under her belt in multiple cities, she is living her purpose of empowering women to share their personal stories. She works closely with each woman, allowing them to explore their vulnerability and gives them the tools they need to shine from the stage.

And it goes beyond the live events. She produces and co-hosts The She Said Project Podcast, visiting with past She Said Speakers and digging into the 'story behind the story.' She co-created and launched the teen empowerment program, "That's What Teens Say," and has personally mentored hundreds of teen girls to stand in their power and share their stories. She has a vision of empowering women everywhere through The She Said Project to uplift each other, build community, and give a voice to stories that need to be told.

So, it made perfect sense that curating a collection of stories and producing this book would be the next step. Born and raised in New Jersey, Jenette made it her business to organize the neighborhood talent shows. Now she can show her parents that it was all part of her master plan. She received her BFA and MBA from the University of Illinois and lived and worked in NY and LA before moving back to Champaign, IL.

Her life would be incomplete without her loves, Brian, Genevieve, and Juliana. She is especially grateful to Josefine, Marie, Frank, Sonia, Libby, Laura, and Monica for the unconditional love and support.

WHAT PEOPLE ARE SAYING ABOUT THAT'S WHAT SHE SAID: FROM THE STAGE TO THE PAGE

This collection of stories filled me with joy, laughter, sadness, heartbreak and hope. The power of She Said in written form is that you can take your time and absorb each word as the story unfolds. The strength of the women who grace these pages is inspiring and their stories are unforgettable. I highly recommend this book.

- Deb Frank Feinen, Mayor of Champaign, IL

Reading this collection of amazing and real stories is self care for the female soul, but all readers are welcome to hear the secrets these brave souls shared. The stories speak to you from the page as well as they did when watching the speaker live performance. I have had the privilege of seeing several of these performances live and it surprised me how much these familiar stories increased in power when I read them.

- Susan Saunders, WBNQ Radio Morning Host & 2021 Bloomington She Said Cast Member

The brave stories in From the Stage to the Page are a testament to the power of autobiography to inspire, connect, and celebrate our resilience. I hope that each reader comes away from the experience feeling nudged a bit closer to believing that their own voice matters and wonders what kind of story they would tell on the "She Said" stage.

- Kate Herald, PhD, TEDxNormal Curator, memoirist, and autobiography researcher

Lightning Source UK Ltd.
Milton Keynes UK
UKHW052007280223
417804UK00001B/18